# THE BEST OF
# THE
# GREAT SMOKY
# MOUNTAINS

## NATIONAL PARK

## A Hiker's Guide to Trails and Attractions

A Tag-Along Book
by Russ Manning and
Sondra Jamieson

Mountain Laurel Place
Norris, Tenn.

Mountain Laurel Place assumes no responsibility or liability for accidents or injuries suffered by persons using this book to explore the Great Smoky Mountains National Park.

*Printed in the United States of America.*

ISBN 0-9625122-2-2

Front Cover:  Gregory Bald
              by Al Foster
Back Cover:  Caldwell Fork Trail
              by Sondra Jamieson

Published by

        Mountain Laurel Place
        P.O. Box 3001
        Norris,  TN     37828

for Grace and Al

who have enriched so many lives

# Acknowledgments

We are grateful to the National Park Service staff of the Great Smoky Mountains National Park for their support in the preparation of this book. Each of the following took the time to meet with us and supply information on the park and its trails: Bob Miller, Management Assistant; Donna Lane, Sales Coordinator and avid Smokies hiker; Glen Cardwell, 30-year Park Ranger who was born in the Greenbrier area of the Smokies; Keny Slay, North District Backcountry Ranger; Keith Nelson, South District Backcountry Ranger; and Paul Williams, Backcountry Ranger. Many others answered our questions in brief telephone interviews.

We also thank Bob Miller, Keny Slay, and Keith Nelson for reviewing our draft manuscript.

# Contents

## Cades Cove Access

## Abrams Creek Access

## Newfound Gap and Clingmans Dome Roads Access

## North Carolina (South District)

## Clingmans Dome and Newfound Gap Roads Access

## Smokemont Access

**The Great Smoky Mountains**

# Mountain and Forest

We both grew up in the flatlands—the coastal plain of southern Alabama and the Mississippi River floodplain of eastern Arkansas. In such monotonous places, the horizon is a straight line, more likely punctuated by a tall tree than a hill.

On our first encounters with mountains, we saw the hills and peaks rising to mysterious heights, creating hidden coves and valleys. We felt the allure of elevation and defile. When we came to live in this mountainous region of East Tennessee and western North Carolina, we found a certain excitement pervading our thoughts because of the proximity of mountains. There is always another region to explore, another peak from which to see this land we now call home.

Of course, the Great Smoky Mountains are the best of this region, an island in the Southern Appalachians where some of the highest peaks in the eastern United States gather to create a highland citadel. The special character of these particular mountains has been recognized by the designation of "national park." In time it has became the most visited national park in the country, with something like 8 million visitors each year.

In spite of the number of visitors, you'll find, as we have, many backcountry trails, some long, some short, that get you away from the crowds. You can wander the mountain ridges and investigate the isolated coves, experiencing for yourself the mystery of the mountains.

As you explore the Smokies, you'll have a particularly rich experience if you pay attention to the natural community around you. The vast deciduous and coniferous forest of these mountains is the special attraction—the trees, the birds, the mammals and reptiles, the shrubs and wildflowers, the mushrooms and toadstools that in season provide a special enjoyment.

In this book, we describe the best trails for wandering the mountains and forests of the Great Smoky Mountains.

Norris, TN                                        Russ Manning and
                                                   Sondra Jamieson

# Park History

At the time the Great Smoky Mountains National Park was established, it was a unique venture. All previous national parks had been formed out of lands already owned by the U.S. Government. To create a national park in the Great Smokies, the land would have to be purchased.

The idea for a national park in the Smokies originated in 1923 with Mr. and Mrs. Willis P. Davis. Willis Davis was at the time manager of the Knoxville Iron Company. After visiting western national parks that summer, the couple thought the Smokies were grand enough for a national park in the East. Others thought it was a good idea too, and a Great Smoky Mountains Conservation Association was established with Davis as president. Col. David C. Chapman, a wholesale druggist in Knoxville, later became the obvious leader through his interest and work in the project and was made chairman of the board.

At the same time, there was talk in Washington about the need for a national park in the South. A Southern Appalachian National Park Committee was sent to investigate. The Smokies Conservation Association met the group in Asheville and induced some members to visit the Smokies. They arrived in August 1924 and were taken to the top of Mt. LeConte where the Association had established a camp. Those committee members were impressed, as were others who came later. So on December 13, 1924, the committee recommended the establishment of two parks, Shenandoah in the Blue Ridge Mountains of Virginia and the Great Smoky Mountains in Tennessee and North Carolina.

In anticipation of a national park being established in the Smokies, a bill was introduced into the Tennessee legislature authorizing purchase of land owned by the Little River Lumber Company. The amended bill called for the City of Knoxville to pay one-third of the purchase price. Knoxville agreed, and the bill was signed in April 1925, but the purchase awaited the intentions of the federal government.

In 1926 a bill passed by the U.S. Congress called for lands to be taken over by the federal government when the States of

North Carolina and Tennessee had purchased at least 150,000 acres and that a national park would be established when a major portion of the land had been secured. The bill was signed by President Calvin Coolidge on May 22, 1926. The Little River property was then purchased in November 1926, the first property to be secured for the park.

The two states accepted the challenge of procuring the land. Park commissions possessing authority to purchase land and to use the right of condemnation were established in both states. Chapman was named chairman of the Tennessee commission, and State Senator Mark Squires headed the North Carolina commission. The two faced a monumental task. The established boundaries encompassed over 6000 separate tracts of land, including large ranges owned by 18 timber and pulpwood companies, more than 1000 small farms, and something like 5000 small lots, some of which had summer homes. In 1926, there were 7300 people living in the designated area.

In addition to overseeing the surveying, appraising, and buying of tracts, the commissions had to raise the necessary money. The funds came from private contributions, including pennies, nickels, and dimes given by schoolchildren; from federal and state government appropriations; and a $5-million gift from the Laura Spelman Rockefeller Memorial, a fund established by John D. Rockefeller, Sr., as a memorial to his wife.

By 1930, purchased land in both states totaled 152,000 acres, the minimum needed for the federal government to accept stewardship. Maj. J. Ross Eakin was named superintendent. Soon the Civilian Conservation Corps began the task of building trails, bridges, and facilities. By 1934 enough land had been purchased and turned over to the federal government that on June 15 the U.S. Congress authorized full establishment of the park. Then on September 2, 1940, the Great Smoky Mountains National Park was dedicated by President Franklin D. Roosevelt as he stood along the curved wall of the Rockefeller Memorial, built at Newfound Gap for the dedication ceremonies.

The 508,000 original acres of the park had been purchased for $12.7 million. The volunteer efforts of hundreds of citizens of Tennessee and North Carolina resulted in a vast forestland being preserved for the enjoyment of the American public.

# Getting There

The Great Smoky Mountains National Park lies amid the Southern Appalachian Mountains. The park straddles the border between Tennessee and North Carolina, half in one state and half in the other.

The Smokies are surrounded by Knoxville to the northwest, Chattanooga to the southwest, Atlanta to the south, Greenville to the southeast, and Asheville to the east. Knoxville and Asheville are the closest—Knoxville for the Tennessee side and Asheville for the North Carolina side—so if you are flying in from another part of the country, you will probably want to arrive at one of these two cities.

The drive from Knoxville is about 30 miles; take I-40 east, get off at the TN66 exit (you'll see signs for the park), and head south through Sevierville, where you'll pick up US441, then through Pigeon Forge and Gatlinburg to the Sugarlands Visitor Center; a bypass takes you around Gatlinburg, but it can be closed in winter. By the end of 1991 a new Gatlinburg Chamber of Commerce building, which will also contain a new park visitor center, will open on a site between Pigeon Forge and Gatlinburg.

The drive from Asheville is about 60 miles; take I-40 west, get off at the US23 exit headed southwest. In about 4 miles bear left on US23/74, the "Great Smoky Mountains Expressway." The highway eventually joins US441 headed north. Stay on 441 through Cherokee and into the park where you'll find the Oconaluftee Visitor Center. You can also get to the North Carolina side of the park along the Blue Ridge Parkway, a 469-mile national scenic highway that connects the Smokies with Shenandoah National Park in Virginia. Sections of the parkway are often closed in winter because of snow and ice.

There are back roads that provide other routes to the park. Although these take longer if you are headed to one of the main entrances at Sugarlands or Oconaluftee, you will probably want to use them if you are headed for a specific access point other than the main entrances. Check highway maps for these alternative routes.

4

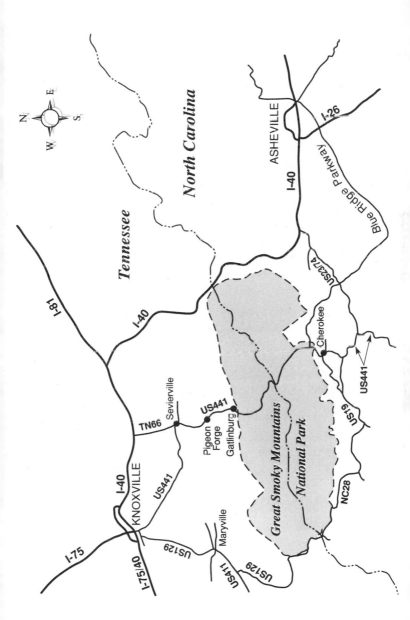

**Getting There**

The two main visitor centers, Sugarlands and Oconaluftee, are connected by 29 miles of US441 that bisects the park. Locally, it is called the "Newfound Gap Road" because it is a transmountain road that crosses the crest of the Smokies at Newfound Gap. At times during the winter, this road is closed to traffic due to snow. In Newfound Gap, you can take the Clingmans Dome Road to the Forney Ridge Parking Area and the trail to the top of Clingmans Dome. This road is closed in winter, usually beginning in mid-November after the first snow and ice.

At the height of the visitor seasons in the spring and fall, and even in summer, the Newfound Gap/Clingmans Dome Roads can be clogged with traffic. In which case, you may want to visit the park at one of the other access points described in this book.

The Foothills Parkway is also under the jurisdiction of the Great Smoky Mountains National Park. The parkway provides scenic vistas along the northern park boundary. There are currently two completed sections of the proposed 72-mile road. A section to the northwest runs from US129 at Chilhowee Lake along the crest of Chilhowee Mountain to US321 near Walland. Along this stretch you'll find the Look Rock observation tower and campground. From the tower, you'll have long views southeast into the park. The other completed section is at the east end of the proposed road and runs from I-40 to US321 near Cosby. This six-mile section has high mountain vistas and so is closed in winter; it offers grand views of the Cosby Area in the park and English Mountain to the northwest outside the park. Construction has been proposed to link these two sections of the parkway by about the year 2000. The right-of-way for this road constitutes around 9,000 acres of the park's 520,000 acres.

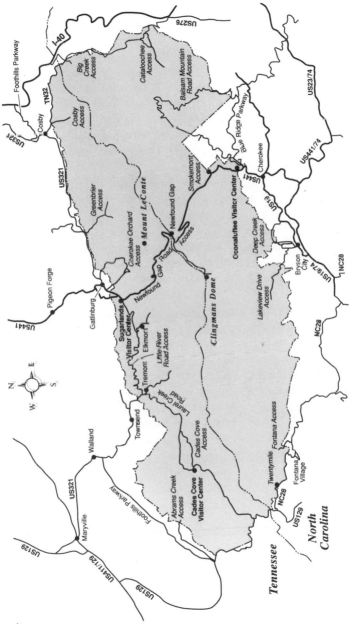

**Access**

7

# Geology

The Appalachians are a long mountain range running northeast to southwest. Hernando DeSoto in 1540 was the first nonnative to see the mountains; he named them "Appalachians," after an Indian tribe he had encountered along the Gulf Coast.

The Southern Appalachians divide into two mountain ranges—the Blue Ridge to the east and the Unakas to the west. At the widest part of the Unaka range stand the Great Smoky Mountains. The Smokies are also the tallest part of the Unakas, with 16 peaks above 6,000 feet where the crest runs from the Pigeon River on the northeast to the Little Tennessee River on the southwest. The waters that gather on the sides of this Smokies crest run north and south and then west to eventually join the Tennessee River that flows westward to the Mississippi River.

At least three mountain ranges have occupied the place where the present Unakas stand today. The building of the mountains began more than a billion years ago with the deposition of the base rock. These oldest rocks were laid down as sediment in a great trough in the earth's crust. After the sediment had accumulated to several thousand feet, the trough closed, possibly because of an early collision of the continental plates that make up the earth's surface. The sedimentary rocks were compressed, broken, folded, and during this time, molten rock from the earth's interior invaded to add heat to the process. The rocks were eventually converted to a hard crystalline mass.

Afterwards, this area was uplifted, probably due again to plate tectonic forces. The land immediately began to erode, with rocks deposited as sediment in a large marine basin to the west. This new deposit solidified about 600 million years ago into rock that became known as the Ocoee Series, made up of the Snowbird, Great Smoky, and Walden Creek Groups.

The Great Smoky Mountains are made up of this Ocoee Series, with the main part of the mountains being the Great Smoky Group within the series. This group is a mass of clastic sedimentary rocks, pebble conglomerate, sandstone, and silty or clay-containing rocks. No fossils are found, primarily due to the ancient age of the rocks. Three formations make up the Great Smoky Group—the fine-grained Elkmont Sandstone on the bottom, the coarse-grained Thunderhead Sandstone in the middle, and the dark silty and clay-containing Anakeesta Formation that has been altered to slate, phyllite, or schist. It is the Anakeesta that forms the steep-sided ridges and pinnacles of the Smokies.

About 450 million years ago, a period of folding and faulting occurred in which the rocks of the Ocoee Series were pushed up and over younger rock to the northwest. Then about 375 million years ago, there followed a period of heat and pressure, and then later more folding and faulting with masses of rock once again being pushed northwest. Then about 250 million years ago there occurred the last episode of great mountain building in which the whole region rose high above sea level.

In the remaining years, the Great Smoky Mountains took shape. The present mountains were not created by the folding and faulting episodes, but by the subsequent erosion that swept away countless tons of rock to leave the mountains you see today. The erosion was perhaps accelerated with additional uplift of the region. The Smokies were once much higher, perhaps higher than the Rocky Mountains, which are younger formations. Erosion has lowered the Smokies, until today there is no treeline as there is in the Rockies because the Smokies no longer stand above the elevation at which trees cannot grow.

From 500,000 to 20,000 years ago, glaciation in the north created colder temperatures in the Great Smokies region. During this period, alternate freezing and thawing caused rock to crack and split into huge boulders that found their way down to the valley floors. You'll find these boulders sitting along streambeds, too big to have been carried there by the action of present or past streams. Once the glaciers retreated and the climate warmed, this action of boulder creation no longer occurred.

Although the Smokies have in the past experienced great faulting and folding and boulder formation, and though occasionally you'll see a rock slide along one of the roads, the mountains today are more settled. They have had millions of years in which to age to rounded mountains clothed in a rich biological diversity.

9

# Plants and Animals

The great attraction of the Great Smoky Mountains is the community of plants and animals. Within this vast forest have been found 1500 species of flowering plants, 100 kinds of trees, 600 mosses, liverworts, and lichens, 2000 different fungi, 50 species of mammals, 80 snakes and amphibians including 22 salamanders, 70 kinds of fish, and 200 different birds. This is probably the most biologically diverse region in all of North America, a feature recognized by its designation as an International Biosphere Reserve under the UNESCO Man in the Biosphere Program.

This biological diversity has an ancient origin. During the Ice Age, northern species of plants gradually moved southward ahead of advancing glaciers. As the temperatures fell, the various northern species invaded as far south as the Smokies. When the Ice Age ended, the glaciers retreated and the northern plant species followed. But all the northern plants did not leave the Smokies region. As the temperatures rose to their original levels, these northern species simply moved up the slopes to the higher, and thus cooler, elevations. As they vacated the lower levels, the southern plant species returned to take their place. As a result, the Great Smoky Mountains have both northern and southern plant species, and a hike from the lowlands to the Smokies crest is often described as a hike from Georgia to Canada because you pass the same plant species along the way.

Today, this great forest can be viewed as five communities of tree associations. The Cove Hardwood Forests occupy the land between the mountain ridges. The trees include basswood, magnolia, white ash, sugar maple, American beech, and silverbell; also present may be buckeye, holly, yellow birch, hemlock, oaks, hickories, red maple, and tulip poplar. It is primarily this forest that produces the spectacular fall color for which the Smokies are known.

Along stream banks and on moist shady slopes stand the Hemlock Forests—cool, dark evergreen forests with a shrub layer of rhododendron, laurel, and doghobble. The Pine-Oak

Forests grow on exposed ridges, which are typically dry. Protected slopes at the higher elevations are occupied by Northern Hardwood Forests, which are dominated by beech and yellow birch and contribute color during the fall season. And at the highest elevations, which get nearly twice as much rainfall as the lowlands, stand the Canadian Spruce-Fir Forests that consist of red spruce and Frasier fir. Found mainly in the national park, the Frasier fir is an allied species of the Balsam fir that grows farther north.

At these highest elevations, there is no treeline. The Smokies are ancient mountains and have already eroded to a level below what would be the treeline for this environment. But there are open areas, called "balds," along some ridges. These can be heath balds, which are covered in shrubs, or grassy balds with a carpet of thick grass and scattered shrubs and small trees.

The forests of the Smokies are the cause of a blue haze that typically hangs over the mountains and gives them their name. The trees through transpiration give off terpenes, hydrocarbon molecules. These terpenes break down in sunlight and recombine to form molecules large enough to refract light and which react with each other and various pollutants to create the blue haze.

The floor of the forest is covered with ferns and mosses, and flowering plants sprinkle the forest with color in spring. Shrubs create an intermediate level in the forest; three of these—rhododendren, mountain laurel, and wild azalea—bloom in late spring and early summer to create a forest wonderland. The ubiquitous rhododendron occurs primarily in two varieties, the Catawba with a rose-purple color and the white Rosebay.

The forest is inhabited by a profusion of wildlife. The chickadee and Carolina wren, the wood thrush, yellow-throated vireo, and hooded warbler, the red-breasted nuthatch, tufted titmouse, and winter wren, and a multitude of other birds occupy the trees and bushes of the forest. You'll occasionally also see owls and woodpeckers and wild turkey and ruffed grouse.

The streams protect the rainbow and brown trout and the native brook trout. Other fish include sculpins, dace, hogsuckers, chubs, shiners, stonerollers, bass, and darters. These live in association with numerous insects, aquatic beetles, spiders, crayfish, leeches and worms, snails, salamanders, and frogs.

**Lady's Slipper**

The mammals occupy both the land and the trees—squirrels, chipmunks, rabbits, mice, skunks, fox, raccoons, opossums. The larger mammals attract the most attention. The numerous white-tailed deer are most easily seen, but the black bear symbolizes the park. The bear population varies from 400 to 600 individuals that can occasionally be seen while hiking or driving one of the park roads.

The park is also inhabited by the wild boar, an exotic that invaded the park after escaping from a hunting preserve in North Carolina. The boar are prolific and now number 1000-2000 in the park. The park staff would like to eradicate the animal because of the damage it does while rooting for food.

Several animals that once lived in the park region are no longer here. Bison became extinct during the time of Indian habitation. Elk were gone by the time of the early pioneers. Wolves were gone soon after the turn of the century.

The cougar was thought to be extinct in the Smokies. But there have been enough recent sightings to convince many that the animal still lives in the park, although hard evidence has not yet been found.

A reintroduction program is underway to return several species to the park. So far, river otters, peregrine falcons, Smoky madtoms, yellowfin madtoms, and spotfin chubs have been reintroduced. Red wolves, one of the most endangered species in the world, are scheduled to be reintroduced the summer of 1991.

The Smokies is one of the last wild areas in the country that is large enough and diverse enough to support such reintroduction programs. At the time the park was established, a third of the forest remained, nearly 150,000 acres, the largest stand of virgin woods in the eastern U.S. In the intervening years, areas that had been severely damaged by farming and logging operations have now recovered.

Although the Smokies are protected from development and abuse with designation as a national park, these forests of the Smokies are threatened. The demise of the chestnut tree is perhaps a harbinger.

The chestnut was once the primary tree of the Great Smoky Mountains. It comprised 20-30 percent of the trees in the park. A parasitic fungus that attacked the chestnut was introduced into

13

**Black Bear**

this country around 1904 and spread throughout the eastern forests. In the 1920s and 1930s, the blight killed the chestnut trees in the park. All that remain are the rotting trunks of fallen trees and occasion sprouts from stumps that eventually die from the blight infestation.

Also at the turn of the century, a balsam woolly adelgid was introduced into this country, an aphid that attacks fir trees. In the Smokies, the adelgid has already killed 90 percent of the adult Frasier firs. As the trees die, other plant species also go; eight species of mosses and liverworts that live in association with the firs are also declining.

Other exotic pests threaten park trees. The dogwood anthracnose, a fungus that is capable of killing the dogwood tree, has now infected 30-40 percent of the park's flowering dogwoods. The gypsy moth, not yet in the park, has destroyed oak forests to the north and is rapidly moving south and will one day invade the park. The hemlock adelgid is also on its way.

In addition, air pollution is causing damage to the park's vegetation. So far 80 plant species show signs of damage from ozone, caused by the reaction of sunlight with pollution in the air. Acid rain is suspected of causing damage to the red spruce of the higher elevations.

The park staff, especially through its Uplands Field Research Laboratory, is working to lessen the effects of these threats to the forests of the Great Smokies. And at least to the extent that they will save a few of each species, they will succeed.

But ultimately, while we try to limit and eradicate exotic pests and work to prevent environmental pollution, we look to nature to adapt. Although the park lost all its chestnut trees 60 to 70 years ago, the forest returned with an increase in other species. The biological diversity ensures that as one species disappears another will take its place, and thus the forest of the Smokies will never disappear. The forest that our grandchildren will see may be different than the forest we know today, but in the Great Smoky Mountains there will always be a forest, for nature will prevail in this last large preserved remnant of the great Southern Appalachian forest.

# Human History

Native Americans once wandered through the mist of the Great Smoky Mountains. By the time white men came to the region, the Cherokees were the Principal People, "Ani-Yunwiya," as they called themselves, "Cherokee" being the white man's name for the People. Their lands covered 40,000 square miles that included the Great Smokies, or as the Indians called it, *Shaconaqe*, "place of blue smoke."

The Cherokees lived by the thousands in villages along streams and rivers, primarily the Little Tennessee River that flows along the southeastern boundary of the present national park. But they ranged far across their lands, following ancient paths, including a transmountain route that crossed the Smokies at Indian Gap, just west of Newfound Gap.

When the white men came to the region, they could not abide such vast lands being left unused, although from the perspective of the Cherokee, the land left in a natural state was well used. Continuous encroachment of white settlers onto Cherokee lands led to numerous battles between the two groups and treaties forced on the Cherokees in which their lands were lost. With the Treaties of 1798 and 1819, the Cherokees were forced to give up the Smoky Mountains, thereafter living to the south and west of the Little Tennessee River.

But treaties were short-lived in those days. With the Indian Removal Acts of 1828 and 1830, pushed through Congress by President Andrew Jackson, the Principal People were told to relinquish all lands and move west of the Mississippi River. In 1838, the U.S. Army received orders to capture those that remained and force them to march to Oklahoma; 4000 Cherokees died along the route that became known as the "Trail of Tears." But before they could all be rounded up, some from the remote villages escaped into the mountains and hid in the coves and hollows of the Smokies. The Army knew it could never capture these Cherokees and so gave up pursuit. In addition there where about 70 Cherokee households who had earlier ceded their lands and so were not included in the eviction orders. These exempt

16

households, along with the escapees, coalesced to become the Eastern Band of the Cherokees, while those that had moved to Oklahoma were the Cherokee Nation, or the Western Band.

During the next ten years, a white man who had been adopted by Chief Yonaguska, William H. Thomas, worked to secure the compensation due the Eastern Band under the treaties. With this compensation, Thomas, who had become de facto chief, purchased some of the Cherokees' former lands to form the Qualla Boundary, named after the principal town in the area, today known simply as the Cherokee Reservation. In 1866, the North Carolina legislature passed an act formally allowing the Cherokees to stay in the state. They were recognized by the U.S. Government in 1868 and officially referred to as the Eastern Band in 1870. Today the Cherokees remain on their reservation at the foot of the Smokies in North Carolina.

With the Cherokees gone from the interior of the Smokies, the mountains were open to settlement. It was still a wild, undeveloped region. The pioneers that had already begun to settle the mountains were primarily "Scotch-Irish," a term applied to Scotsmen who relocated to Ireland in the early 1600s and whose descendants then began a migration to America in the early 1700s. They first settled the Pennsylvania region, but then moved south through Virginia into the Carolinas. They joined with Germans and English to penetrate the mountains that were first officially referred to as the "Smoaky Mountains" in the Act of 1789 when North Carolina offered to cede to the federal government its western lands, which became the Southwest Territory and eventually the State of Tennessee. The mountain range was also at one time called the "Great Iron Mountains."

The people moved up the coves and into the river valleys of the mountains. They cut trees to build log cabins and open fields. This was still a primeval forest with trees so large many could not be cut. So the settlers often girdled the trees so they would die and thus let the sun reach the forest floor where the farmers then planted corn, the primary crop. They were a self-sufficient people who gathered nuts and berries and hunted wild game, as well as cultivating crops and raising hogs and chickens.

Many of these early settler families lived alone in their coves, widely separated from their nearest neighbors. But in

**Pioneer Farmstead**

places, communities grew along water courses and in fertile coves. Oconaluftee and Cades Cove were settled first; the largest concentrations were in Greenbrier Cove and the Sugarland and Cataloochee Valleys. In such places, the people banded together to form communities with schools and churches.

Apart from this settlement by hardy mountaineers, the mountains remained essentially undisturbed. But it was inevitable that the forest resources would attract the attention of the outside world. Lumber companies learned of the mammoth trees and unending forests of the Smokies. The companies moved into the mountains, bought land, and began cutting roads and laying rail lines to haul out the trees. Among the several companies, the Little River Lumber Company on the Tennessee side and the Champion Fibre Company on both sides of the mountains were the largest. Company towns were built to house the workers, places like Smokemont, Tremont, and Elkmont. With the felling of the trees, some so massive a single tree filled a railcar, the mountains were devastated by erosion and fire.

It's easy from the perspective of the late 20th century to characterize these men and their companies as exploiters and despoilers of the land, which they were. And perhaps the lumber barons can be blamed for their "cut and get out" attitudes. But from the perspective of the early part of the century, the men who manned the logging camps were hard workers who supplied a needed resource for the building of homes and towns and cities in a fast-growing country.

But whatever the view, few if any will now argue that it was fortunate the movement to create a national park began at a time when approximately 150,000 acres of the primeval forest could be saved. These now make up the virgin stands in the Smokies. In the intervening years the forest has returned in the logged areas so that now a half million acres of forest clothe the mountains.

No one lives in the Great Smoky Mountains any longer, except in the surrounding valleys and on the opposing hillsides beyond the park boundaries. Yet this is a place many visit and then return to time and again, drawn back by some sense of belonging. Millions come each year to find their stamina challenged, their minds cleared, and their spirits replenished in an act many characterize as "coming home."

# Wilderness

In 1965, the Director of the National Park Service recommended a second transmountain road through the Great Smoky Mountains National Park. Conservationists were opposed and worked for years to discourage proposals for roads that would destroy the integrity of the park. Although there are no current road proposals and the present park administration is dedicated to preserving park lands, there is no guarantee that a new road through the park will not be proposed once again.

To permanently protect the Great Smoky Mountains, conservationists for more than a decade have called for wilderness designation under the National Wilderness Preservation System. Approximately 475,000 acres of the park qualify for wilderness protection. These are the lands of deep forest and high mountain, crossed only by the trails described in this guide. All lands in the park with current development are excluded from the wilderness proposal. So the designation of these acres as wilderness would not change existing use by visitors; it would only prevent damage to the park by further development. The current park administration supports wilderness designation.

Although legislation has twice been introduced to the U.S. Congress to designate most of the national park as wilderness, the effort has stalled over a 1943 agreement in which the NPS accepted a 44,000-acre addition to the park in trade for the promise to build a road within the park along the north shore of the Fontana Reservoir. The road was never built, and now most people are opposed to the building of a road. A payment to Swain County, the principal county involved, has been proposed in lieu of a road, but there are some in North Carolina who still want the road built. In addition, there are those who simply oppose wilderness for the park lands.

Conservationists persist in the work for official wilderness designation to protect for all time this last great mountain wilderness in the eastern United States. If you want to add your voice to the call for wilderness, contact the Conservation Committee of the Smoky Mountains Hiking Club.

# Hiking

There are 850 miles of trails in the Great Smoky Mountains National Park. Many are both horse and hiking trails; but many are just for walking. From this large number of trails, we have picked the best to describe in this book, although our "best" is a subjective opinion. If we have left out your favorite, let us know and we will consider it for an expanded and updated edition.

We've divided the book into Tennessee and North Carolina sections and arranged the trails so you can hike all the Tennessee trails and then take the Newfound Gap Road, hiking trails along the way, to the North Carolina side for the trails on that side of the mountains. If you approach the park from the North Carolina side, you will probably want to hike the trails on that side of the mountains first before taking the Newfound Gap Road to the Tennessee side. Of course, you can skip around and hike the trails in any order you would like.

The Tennessee side is presented first because more people arrive at the park on that side of the mountains; it also has the park headquarters at the Sugarlands Visitor Center and, just outside the park, the resort towns of Gatlinburg and Pigeon Forge. But because most people arrive on the Tennessee side, that has left the North Carolina side less developed and more isolated, and so some might say, the better half of the park.

In addition, the trails are grouped by access point. So when you arrive at an access, you'll find the descriptions of trails from that access assembled in one section.

The best times to hike the Great Smoky Mountains are spring and fall, when the temperatures are mild and you have the special attraction of either abundant wildflowers or a forest of red and gold. But in winter, you get to experience the snow-covered mountains, and even at the height of summer, you can find cool coves in the depths of the forest.

You might want to time some of your visits to coincide with festivals held in the park. The last weekend in April is the Great Smoky Mountains Wildflower Pilgrimage in which you can join guided walks for flower identification and other natural history

**Spring Wildflower Pilgrimage**

topics. Cades Cove has gatherings at the Cable Mill area—Old Timers Day in May and September, Storytelling in June, and a Quilt Show in July. Fontana Village sponsors both a spring wildflower hiking week and a fall color hiking week.

## Trail Descriptions

The hikes we describe in this guide range from short walks to long backpacking trails. For those who prefer short hikes, we have even with many of the long trails given the distance to an attraction part way along the trail that can be your destination.

The trail numbers correspond to the numbers on the accompanying maps. Once at the trailhead, you should be able to find your way by using our descriptions and the signs along the trails. *But we expect you assume responsibility for knowing where you are going and for not getting lost.* Be aware that, with the exception of the Appalachian Trail, the trails in the Smokies are not blazed, although it's usually easy to see where the footpaths go. Always let someone know where you are going and give them an expected return time so someone can contact park authorities if you don't show up. To keep from getting lost, read trail signs, stay on the trails, and don't over estimate your ability. Hiking in the mountains can be difficult because of the distances and steep terrain; hikers often under estimate the difficulty and so also under estimate the time required to cover a trail. If you do get lost, do not leave the trail; search teams will cover the trails first when looking for you.

For each of the hikes in this book, we have given the distance (note that the mileages are always cumulative) and rating of easy, moderate, or difficult. This rating is based on a somewhat subjective judgment of the strenuousness of the trail—how much up and down there is, how difficult are the stream crossings, whether the footing on the trail is rocky. As a result, while a 10-mile trail would be difficult for anyone not used to hiking, it might be rated easy if it is relatively level, has no creek crossings, and is fairly easy walking. So if you are not accustomed to hiking, look not only at the degree of difficulty, but also at the distance you will walk (double that if the trail does not form a loop; you'll also have to walk back) and notice the particular precautions you must take on the trail.

We have based our degree of difficulty on the ability of an average person, someone who hikes occasionally but for whom a walk ascending a thousand feet or more is not a frequent occurrence. So more experienced hikers may find many of the moderate hikes quite easy and the difficult hikes fairly moderate. Someone who rarely hikes will find the moderate and perhaps the easy trails difficult.

The elevation "gain" or "loss" we give for a trail indicates a difference in elevation between the trail's beginning and end. Be aware that there could be several ups and downs along the way; so while walking a trail that gains or loses 1000 feet, you could ascend and descend a total of many more feet. Then of course, if you backtrack to your starting point, you will cover that same elevation fluctuation again.

We use elevation "change" to indicate the difference between the lowest and highest points on a loop trail, because if you are walking a loop, you will gain and lose the same elevation during the hike. We also use "change" when the hike is one way but the trail climbs through a pass and then descends; in that case the highest point is along the trail, not at the beginning or end, and you both ascend and descend while hiking the trail just one way.

For those of you who wish to walk farther, we have included trail connections so you may combine several trails for longer walks. Many of these combinations can be used to form loop hikes, but most get to be quite long, so you need to be in good shape for walking the total mileage or plan on camping in the backcountry to make a two- or three-day trip out of it. The numbered campsites along a given trail are also listed.

Although we have described in detail only some of the park trails, we discuss virtually every trail when giving directions at trail junctions. To help in making these trail connections, we have also included a trail index in the back so you can easily find the pages on which a specific trail and its connections are discussed, including trails not specifically described in this book.

**Preparations**

Even if you are out for only a short walk, you should wear walking shoes or hiking boots, which are designed to give sure footing and to support ankles. For day hikes in which you intend to be out more than an hour or two, carry along water, a lunch or snacks, and rain gear; it rains frequently in the Great Smoky Mountains. You should also take along a first aid kit and a map and compass; and just in case you get lost, bring along extra clothes, a knife, a flashlight, and a lighter or waterproof matches plus some firestarter for building a fire. If you do get lost or need to make an injured person comfortable, you'll also be glad you brought along a plastic sheet or emergency blanket.

If you are backpacking, you of course need everything for surviving in the open overnight and for however many days you choose to be out. If you are inexperienced in backpacking, the park rangers or your local outfitters can give advice on the equipment needed.

If you want more detailed information than our book provides on the terrain you are to cover, you'll need to check the topographical maps that cover the area you will be hiking. Our maps are designed to help you in finding the trailheads and showing the general route and trail connections; they do not provide for detailed navigating. You must have topographical maps if you intend to hike cross country. Topographical maps are available from your local map supplier and at the park visitor centers. At the minimum, whether dayhiking or backpacking, you should have the inexpensive "Great Smoky Mountains Trail Map," available at visitor centers and various other places throughout the park; the map gives you an overall view of the trails and their connections.

The park rangers recommend that you plan ahead. So read through the descriptions in this book prior to going, plan your route, and study the trail connections while looking at an overall map of the park. The park rangers will be glad to give you additional information about a trail and the current conditions.

## Precautions

You'll occasionally see horses on trails designated as both hiking and horse trails. But pets, bicycles, motorized vehicles, and guns are not allowed in the backcountry. Hunting is not allowed anywhere in the park.

While you are out there, take care of the park. Do not pick the wildflowers and leave historic and archaeological sites undisturbed. Take care of yourself as well; be especially careful climbing on rocks, walking along the edge of bluffs, and crossing streams. Don't even think of climbing on waterfalls. We mention such situations in the trail descriptions, but we cannot mention every place you should be careful. *So we expect you to take responsibility for your own safety, keeping in mind that hiking in a wilderness setting far from medical attention is an inherently hazardous activity.* It is best to hike with someone. Then if a person in your party is injured, someone will be there to care for the injured person. If the injured cannot make it back to the trailhead, make the person warm and comfortable, leave someone to tend the person if there is a third hiker in your party, pay attention to the exact location, and then hike out and contact the park rangers who will go back to rescue the injured.

Time was, you could kneel and drink from pristine springs in the Smokies. But with more and more people in the backcountry, horses along the trails, and wild boar that wallow in the streams, that time is quickly fading into memory. All water in the backcountry should be considered contaminated. Boil water at least one minute before drinking to destroy bacteria and other microorganisms, including Giardia, a flagellate protozoan causing an intestinal disorder called "Giardiasis." There are also filters and water purifying tablets that can be purchased, but ask your supplier for ones that indeed remove Giardia.

The Smoky Mountains have snakes, including the northern copperhead and the timber rattler. To be safe, simply watch where you put your feet, and if you must walk through high brush and weeds, explore ahead with a stick. We have encountered several snakes in our years of hiking the mountains, but have yet to see one of the poisonous species. If you do encounter snakes, leave them alone; they belong here.

During the warm spring and summer days, the gnats, ticks, and mosquitoes can be a bother. We have seen more than our share of these. In summer, you might carry along insect repellant for when the gnats and mosquitoes become incessant.

Before starting off on a hike, spray your shoetops, socks, legs, and pants with repellant to discourage ticks, one type of which, the deer tick, can transmit a spirochete that causes Lyme disease. Although Lyme disease is still rare in the southeastern

26

states, you should remain very conscious of keeping ticks off you and checking for ticks after a hike.

And there is poison ivy. If you stay to the trails, you'll probably not come into contact with any. If you do venture off trail or encounter an overgrown trail, watch for the three-leaf clusters. You might also encounter stinging nettle, a foot-high plant that has stinging hairs; if you brush against it, you'll feel the stinging for several minutes, but with no lasting effects.

Stream crossings can be quite easy or quite difficult. After a heavy rain, a stream can be swollen with rushing water. Do not attempt to cross such a stream unless you are sure you can make it. When the water level is down, you'll find that you can rockhop most streams, but this can also be hazardous if the rocks are wet and/or moss covered; use caution and be prepared to slip. If you decide to wade across, wear your shoes to protect your feet; some hikers carry along old tennis shoes to slip into for stream crossings. Find a stick to use for balance. If you are carrying a pack, release the hip belt so you can easily slip out of the pack if you fall in the water. If you do take a dunking and the water carries you away, orient yourself to float on your back with your feet downstream so you can ward off rocks until you have a chance to stop yourself and get out of the water. Even when you are crossing a footbridge over a creek you should use caution. Some of the bridges are long and narrow and can be wet and slippery or in winter covered with ice.

Weather in the mountains can become a problem; so dress appropriately, preferably in layers so you can adjust your clothes as you warm up or cool down. It rains frequently, and so you should always have rain gear. It can also be quite cold; you may find snow on the ground and/or freezing conditions in the high elevations when the conditions are relatively mild in the lowlands. So be prepared. Once we were on a backpack during a heat wave in the middle of summer, but when the sun went down, the temperature dropped and we shivered all night in our summer sleeping bags, even after putting on all our clothes.

Besides the uncomfortableness of being wet and cold, you also face the danger of hypothermia, the lowering of core temperature beyond the point at which the body can maintain its own heat. The symptoms are uncontrolled shivering, slurred speech,

27

memory lapse, stumbling, fumbling hands, and drowsiness. Hypothermia can occur in any season and can result in death. Since it is caused by being wet and cold, the treatment is to get dry and warm. If you are wet and cold, get under some shelter and change into dry clothes. If you begin to experience symptoms, get in a sleeping bag, if available. Drink warm fluids to raise the core temperature of your body. We have heard of hikers who, beginning to feel the symptoms of hypothermia, began running to increase their body heat, but this should only be attempted in the early stages when you are coherent. To prevent hypothermia from occurring, stay dry, eat even if you are not hungry so your body will have fuel from which to produce heat energy, and drink water even when you are not thirsty so your body can assimilate your food.

The wild boar is a nonnative species in the park. They are nocturnal and so are seldom seen by hikers. If you do encounter a herd of boar, simply stand still. The boar will probably be more scared of you than you are of them. In fact, in their frenzy to run away, they will scatter in all directions; if you also try to run away, the two of you might collide.

Bears are the primary mammal in the park that can pose a threat to humans, but these are black bears and not nearly so dangerous at the grizzlies that inhabit the western parks. Even so, you should take precautions to not attract or irritate the bears. A mother bear is very protective of her cubs. If you encounter a mother with cubs, or a cub alone whose mother is surely nearby, back off. Do not advance on the bears and do not place yourself between the mother and her cubs. We once looked up to see a cub climbing a tree; we did not wait around to see if the cub was just having fun or if its mother had scooted it up the tree thinking we were a danger. We quickly moved on, keeping an eye on the surrounding woods.

If you face a lone bear, observe from a distance; do not turn and run, which might cause the bear to run after you. But back off, if you must, to avoid an encounter. On that same hike, we encountered a larger bear at about twenty yards; it was a beautiful animal with thick black fur. After staring at the bear and him staring back for some time, one of us spoke to him in a quiet voice, and he turned and high-tailed it up the ridge.

28

Under no circumstances should you feed a bear or leave food for a bear, who would then learn that people carry food and so pose a threat to hikers that come after you. You should also avoid attracting the bears with your food. Once after passing west over Thunderhead Mountain, we were strolling through Spence Field when a huge bear sat up from where it was resting in the shade of a tree. It was a hot summer day, and the bear decided we were not worth the bother and just watched us pass by. Later in the day, we met a couple who said they had apparently encountered the same bear, and it had proved to be quite aggressive after they sat down and opened a can of tunafish for lunch.

Don't be discouraged from walking the trails by all these warnings. Many people have walked these mountains before you and only a relative few have suffered injuries. Just be prepared and use common sense. Getting to see the Great Smoky Mountains is well worth having to take a few precautions.

### Nature Trails

You'll find a number of quiet walkways scattered along the thoroughfares in the park. There are also several easy, short walks, including designated self-guiding nature trails where you'll find interpretive fliers in stands at the trailheads for most. Also, some of the trails described in this book start with relatively brief walks to scenic attractions, which we often list in parentheses in the trail features.

If you are beginner to hiking, these walkways, brief walks, and nature trails are where you should start. You can loosen up on these short trails while experiencing the mountain forest and then begin to build your stamina on the easy trails described in this guide. Someday soon you'll find yourself atop Mt. LeConte.

The one-mile *Sugarlands Nature Trail* begins behind the Sugarlands Visitor Center. On the west side of the building you'll see a paved walk that soon splits, with the Gatlinburg Trail to the right and the nature trail to the left. The trail wanders through part of a lowland, called "Sugarlands" because of the sugar maples that once grew in the area. Unfortunately most of the maples were cut during the lumbering years. The loop walk takes you by the restored John Ownby cabin.

Although not a designated nature trail, the 2.1-mile one-way *Gatlinburg Trail* provides an easy walk connecting Gatlinburg with the Sugarlands Visitor Center. Begin at the same place where the Sugarlands Nature Trail begins. The right fork is the Gatlinburg Trail that leads by the park headquarters, then along a road to the left for 0.2 mile, and then to the right into the woods along the West Prong of the Little Pigeon River and US441 out of Gatlinburg. Before reaching the town, the trail crosses the West Prong on a bridge. Of course you can also start at the Gatlinburg end of the trail, which begins past the last building in town just inside the park boundary on the west side of US441.

The three-quarter-mile *Noah "Bud" Ogle Nature Trail* begins on the Cherokee Orchard Road. Take Airport Road southeast at traffic light #8 in Gatlinburg. The road becomes Cherokee Orchard Road in 0.6 mile. Parking for the nature trail is at 2.7 miles. The trail takes you through the farm of Bud Ogle, established in 1879. The place was called "Junglebrook" because of the jungle of rhododendron and magnolia.

The mile-long *Cosby Nature Trail* wanders through the stream environment of Cosby Creek, passing over the creek and its tributaries on footbridges. The nature trail begins on the left in the Cosby Campground after passing the small camping registration hut and across from a ranger residence.

The 1.3-mile, one-way, paved path to *Laurel Falls*, located 3.7 miles west of the Sugarlands Visitor Center on the Little River Road, is a designated nature trail; you'll pass through a pine-oak forest to Laurel Falls. (See trail description #14.)

The three-quarter-mile *Elkmont Nature Trail* is located 4.9 miles west from the Sugarlands Visitor Center on Little River Road. Turn left into Elkmont and in 1.3 miles turn left just before entering the Elkmont campground, and in another 0.3 mile, you'll find parking on the left. The trail guides you up the valley of Mids Branch where a spur line of the Little River Railroad once hauled logs out of the mountains.

The one-mile one-way *Little Greenbrier School Trail* leads from the Metcalf Bottoms Picnic Area on Little River Road to the Little Greenbrier School. The 1882 log building was used as a school and a Primitive Baptist Church until 1935. After turning into the picnic area, you'll find the beginning of the trail on the
30

right just after crossing the bridge over the Little River. You can also drive to the schoolhouse by continuing up the Wear Cove Road for about one mile to a narrow gravel road to the right that leads to the school and a cemetery.

The half-mile *Cades Cove Nature Trail*, located 6.3 miles along the Cades Cove Loop Road, guides you through a woodland environment where you'll learn how the settlers of Cades Cove used native plants.

Also in Cades Cove, you can walk the three-quarter-mile *Vista Trail* that offers a view of the cove. In the campground, you'll find the start of the trail between and across the road from campsites C-14 and C-15. You'll just see a path into the woods; there is no sign. There's little parking here, so if you are not staying in the campground, you should probably park in the lot by the ranger station and walk into the campground. The trail forms a loop that takes you up to a knoll from which you have a long distance, porthole view through the trees.

The three-quarter-mile *Cove Hardwood Nature Trail*, located just inside the entrance to the Chimney Tops Picnic Area 4.4 miles south of the Sugarlands Visitor Center on Newfound Gap Road, guides you through second-growth woods where farming once occurred into a mature cove hardwood forest where you'll see samples of large trees.

The 2.5-mile one-way *Alum Cave Nature Trail* is the longest and most difficult of the nature trails; this should not be your first walk if you are not used to hiking. The trailhead is 8.6 miles south of the Sugarlands Visitor Center on Newfound Gap Road. On the trail, you'll climb 1000 feet, passing through Arch Rock and along a heath bald to Alum Cave. (See trail description #33.)

The half-mile *Spruce/Fir Nature Trail* is 2.6 miles along the Clingmans Dome Road from its beginning at Newfound Gap. The clockwise loop walk takes you through a forest of red spruce and Frasier fir typical of the higher elevations in the park. If you catch it when a cloud envelops the mountain, it's a magical place.

Although not a designated nature trail, the half-mile one-way paved path to *Clingmans Dome*, although steep, is a route that is easily walked if you stop to get your breath once in a while. Take the Clingmans Dome Road out of Newfound Gap to its end. From the observation tower crowning this highest

31

mountain in the park, you'll have a 360-degree view of the Great Smoky Mountains.

The three-quarter-mile, one-way *Smokemont Nature Trail* starts in the Smokemont Campground on the Newfound Gap Road, 3.1 miles north of the Oconaluftee Visitor Center or 12.4 miles south of Newfound Gap. When you enter the campground, turn left after crossing the Oconaluftee River and then keep right past the check-in station to the second left through the campsites. On the other side of the campground turn left and watch for parking near a bridge over Bradley Fork. This is also the beginning of the Smokemont Loop (see trail description #44). The nature trail follows an old road that parallels the Oconaluftee River. If you continue straight past the right turn up the hill along the Smokemont Loop, you'll soon come to a path on the right up to the old Bradley Cemetery. At the back of the cemetery, you'll find a path that leads up to the Smokemont Loop where you can take a right to return to your starting point.

The 1.5-mile one-way *Mingus Creek Road* offers a moderate walk to an old cemetery. Start at the Mingus Mill historic place half a mile north up Newfound Gap Road from the Oconaluftee Visitor Center. The rehabilitated turbine mill with millrace and flume was originally constructed in 1886 to replace an older mill that had been built here by John Jacob Mingus when he settled the region in the 1790s. After visiting the mill, take the gravel road at the end of the parking area into the woods for a stroll along Mingus Creek. In 0.3 mile you'll pass a shooting range; this road has no admittance when the range is in use. You'll pass a water treatment station after the firing range, and at 1.0 mile a path to the left that is the old Mingus Creek Trail. Stay with the road to the right. The creek crossings all have footbridges except one small stream that you can hop without much difficulty.

At the Oconaluftee Visitor Center, you can pick up the 1.5 mile one-way *Oconaluftee River Trail* that wanders along the Oconaluftee River to end at the Cherokee Reservation outside the park. From the visitor center, walk down toward the Pioneer Farmstead, a re-creation of a pioneer farm using a collection of authentic log structures. The river trail actually begins just as you reach the farmstead. Turning right, the trail, which appears as a jeep road, skirts the compound and then enters the woods on a

32

**Mingus Mill**

graveled trail. Following along the river, you'll see a display of wildflowers in spring, among them purple phacelia, phlox, mayapple, toothwort, foam flower, trillium, and violets.

The three-quarter-mile *Balsam Mountain Nature Trail* starts at the Balsam Mountain Campground near the end of the Balsam Mountain Road. The walk exposes you to the sites and sounds of a forest of northern hardwoods and spruce-fir.

In the Deep Creek area, in addition to short walks to Tom Branch and Indian Creek Falls, you can also take a half-mile one-way walk to *Juneywhank Falls* on Juneywhank Branch. At 0.4 mile past the Deep Creek Campground on the Deep Creek Road, you'll see a sign on the left directing you to the waterfall. The path climbs from the road; on the way you'll pass a horse trail leading off to the right which is part of the Deep Creek Horse Trail system that keeps the horses off the Deep Creek Road. At the falls, a picturesque cascade in the descent of Juneywhank Branch toward Deep Creek, a path leads down to a footbridge across the base of the falls.

The half-mile one-way paved path to *Look Rock* on the Foothills Parkway offers a little climb. Drive the parkway section between US321 and US129 at the northwest corner of the park. You'll find parking for Look Rock about 10 miles from the US321 end and about 8 miles from the US129 end. The path begins across the road at the east end of the parking area. From the lookout tower atop Chilhowee Mountain, you'll have a grand view of the Smokies Crest to the southeast.

## Camping

There are several established fee campgrounds in the park that are accessible by automobile. Reservations are recommended for May 15 to October 31 for the Cades Cove, Elkmont, and Smokemont Campgrounds; call your local Ticketron office. You can just show up and be given an open campsite, but it's not likely there will be one. All other campgrounds (Cosby, Abrams Creek, Big Creek, Cataloochee, Balsam Mountain, Deep Creek, and Look Rock) are first come, first served. The Cades Cove, Elkmont, and Smokemont Campgrounds are open all year; during the winter and early spring, they are first come, first served. All other campgrounds are closed in winter. In addition,
34

there is LeConte Lodge that provides meals and lodging in the backcountry at the top of Mt. LeConte. The only access to the lodge is a hike of several miles. You must have a reservation.

You may camp for free in the backcountry at designated campsites, which are indicated by campsite number, and at established shelters; camping in the backcountry is not allowed anywhere else. For your own safety and to protect the park resources, you must register for a campsite prior to beginning your hike. You will be subject to a fine if caught camping without a registration or if you are found in an undesignated site. For most campsites, you may self-register at any of the ranger stations, visitor centers, and campgrounds around the park and also at Fontana Dam. You may also register in person with a ranger. At the Sugarlands Visitor Center, volunteers are available Spring through Labor Day to help with backcountry planning and registration; since this is the busy season, you might phone ahead. Some of the campsites (nos. 10, 13, 23, 24, 29, 36, 37, 38, 47, 50, 55, 57, 61, 71, and 83) and all shelters are rationed, and so you must contact the Backcountry Reservation Office (615/436-1231) to reserve a place at one of these areas. To ensure you get a place, you may call up to a month in advance.

You may stay up to three consecutive nights at a campsite but only one night at a shelter. When you are staying at a shelter, you must use the shelter and not pitch a tent. You are subject to a fine if found in a tent beside a shelter. You may use down timber for campfires at designated spots at the campsites.

In the backcountry, all food and trash must be hung from a tree to keep it away from bears. Use a long rope over two limbs to suspend your pack or food and trash bags at least ten feet from the ground and four feet from any tree or limb (refer to the park's Great Smoky Mountains Trail Map for an illustration). Occasionally the campsites have storage devices for storing your food securely. Most shelters are bear proof, and so you should keep your food in those shelters with you. Also to avoid encounters, keep cooking and sleeping areas separate, except at shelters. Also, keep your tent and sleeping bags free of food odors by not putting food in them. If you have hung only your food and trash bags, keep your pack and boots inside the tent with you when you retire.

For water, you'll find a spring or creek near most campsites, but at least within half a mile of all sites. We assume you'll be carrying water with you during the day and so we do not point out sources of drinking water along the trails, although you can of course get water from the numerous streams and creeks that the trails cross. But be aware that water sources we describe as seeps, trickles, small streams, and even some streams may be dry certain times of the year. Boil all drinking water.

Bury your waste at least six inches deep away from trails, water sources, and campsites. Do not bury sanitary napkins and tampons; instead add them to your trash bag and carry them out. Do not wash dishes or bathe in a stream; take water from the streams to do your washing and let the waste water drain onto the ground. Pack out all trash and litter.

## Appalachian Trail

For 2100 miles the Appalachian Trail travels from Mt. Katahdin, Maine, to Springer Mountain, Georgia. The "AT," as it is commonly referred to, is the longest completed trail in the country and one of the longest in the world. It was the first national scenic trail to be designated in the United States.

For 68 of those many miles, the AT passes through the Great Smoky Mountains National Park, for the most part following along the crest of the Smokies that is also the dividing line between the states of Tennessee and North Carolina. The trail enters the park at Davenport Gap at the northeast end of the park and travels the mountain ridge through the park, until at Doe Knob it turns down the mountain to exit the park at Fontana Dam on the southwest.

Because the AT follows the Smokies crest, it offers some of the best views in the park. We do not discuss the entire AT in our trail descriptions, but we do take you to some of the more interesting spots, such as Mt. Cammerer, Charlies Bunion, Silers Bald, Thunderhead Mountain, and the Shuckstack. In the spring along these sections of the AT, you'll often see "through hikers," those headed north to Maine or as far as they can walk. If you are staying overnight in one of the shelters on the AT, save the best spot for these hardy souls; they have already come a long way and have an exceedingly long way yet to go.

## Adopt-a-Trail Program

If you live in the area of the Great Smokies or visit frequently and would like to participate in maintaining the park's many trails, you may want to join the Adopt-a-Trail Program. This is a volunteer program in which participants hike a specific trail a minimum of ten times a year to perform routine minor trail maintenance and to report to the park staff on trail conditions, hazards, signs, and any emergency actions needed. You will attend a four-hour orientation session before conducting your first trail patrol.

So if you are at least 18 years old and in good physical condition and would like to adopt a trail, contact the park headquarters at the address and phone number listed in the back of this book.

## Bicycling

You may, as we do, occasionally add diversity to your outings by bicycling or sometimes using bikes to shuttle from one end of a hike to the other. Bicycles are not allowed on trails in the park, even when the trails are old roads that see a lot of horse traffic. But you can take bicycles anywhere motorized vehicles are allowed, although many park roads are unsuitable for bicycling.

Some back roads that see less traffic and so are good for recreational bicycling are the roads in the Greenbrier Access off US321, the mostly one-way Rich Mountain Road connecting Cades Cove with Townsend, the one-way Heintooga/Round Bottom Road out of the Balsam Mountain Access, the roads in Cataloochee Valley, and the road into Elkmont off the Little River Road and the road into Tremont just west of the Townsend Wye. These are all or partially gravel, and so you should probably use an all-terrain bicycle or a street/all-terrain hybrid. And always wear a helmet.

A special treat is to bike the 11-mile Cades Cove Loop Road, but the volume of traffic can often be intimidating. Fortunately, the park staff has set aside Saturday mornings until 10:00 a.m. for bikers; the road is closed to motorized vehicles until that time. So get there early and enjoy some quiet, leisurely bicycling.

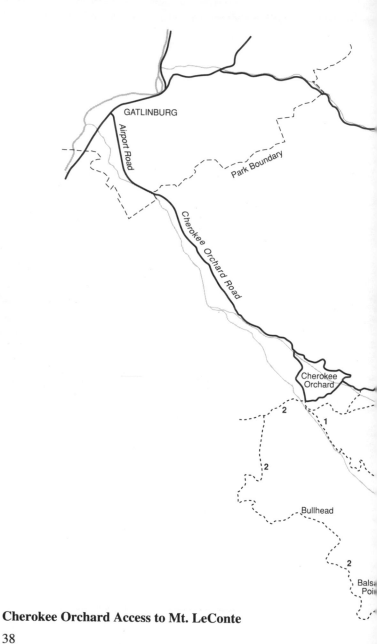

**Cherokee Orchard Access to Mt. LeConte**

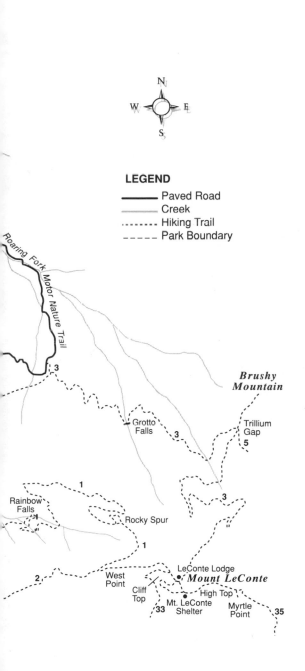

LEGEND

——— Paved Road
——— Creek
········ Hiking Trail
– – – – Park Boundary

N
W E
S

Roaring Fork Motor Nature Trail

3

Brushy Mountain

Grotto Falls

3

Trillium Gap

5

1

Rainbow Falls

1

Rocky Spur

1

2

West Point

Cliff Top

LeConte Lodge

Mount LeConte

High Top

3

Mt. LeConte Shelter

33

Myrtle Point

35

# 1 Rainbow Falls Trail

6.0 miles one way
(Rainbow Falls 2.6 miles one way)
(LeConte Lodge 6.6 miles one way)
Difficult
Elevation Gain: 4000 ft.
Cautions: Continuous ascent, narrow footbridges
Campsites: LeConte Lodge, Mt. LeConte Shelter
Connections: Bullhead, Trillium Gap, Alum Cave,
Boulevard Trails

**Attractions**: This trail leads by Rainbow Falls to the summit of Mt. LeConte and LeConte Lodge, one of the most popular park destinations. This is one of five routes to Mt. LeConte.

**Trailhead**: The Rainbow Falls Trail begins at the Cherokee Orchard Access. Take Airport Road southeast out of Gatlinburg at traffic light #8. It soon becomes Cherokee Orchard Road, and you'll cross the boundary into the national park at 0.9 mile. At 2.0 miles you'll pass the road on the right to the Uplands Field Research Laboratory that conducts studies in the park's ecosystem processes and evaluates the status of threatened species. You'll pass by the Noah "Bud" Ogle homesite at 2.7 miles and then encounter a fork where you'll bear right on a one-way loop. You'll find parking for the Rainbow Falls Trail on the right at 3.4 miles. Cherokee Orchard Road is the beginning of a scenic drive that continues on the 6-mile Roaring Fork Motor Nature Trail, which is closed in winter. Along the one-way route, you'll pass by scenic overlooks and preserved remnants of the farms and homes which once dotted the Roaring Fork Community that existed around the turn of the century. The road comes out on Low Gap Road that leads to US321 on the east end of Gatlinburg.

**Description**: From the trailhead parking, walk to the right into the woods; you'll soon encounter trail junction signs with the Rainbow Falls Trail straight ahead. To the left is a connecting
40

trail to the beginning of the Trillium Gap Trail, and to the right is a short trail to the beginning of the Bullhead Trail.

The Rainbow Falls Trail immediately begins ascending the flank of Mt. LeConte while paralleling LeConte Creek, which pours down from the highlands. The stream was once called "Mill Creek," for all the grist mills that were located along its banks for grinding corn into meal. Most, if not all, were tub mills, first brought to the U.S. by Swedes when they settled in Delaware. A tub mill had a vertical shaft with millstones on top and paddles forming a waterwheel on the bottom; the wheel was enclosed in a tub that increased the efficiency by about 10 percent because of the weight of water that was carried around inside the tub before spilling out a hole in the bottom. There were hundreds of these mills scattered throughout the Smokies at one time. You can see the remains of one at the Noah "Bud" Ogle farm.

As you continue up the Rainbow Falls Trail, you'll find the trail swings away from the creek and then loops back to cross the creek on a footbridge at about 1.5 miles. You'll then climb through several switchbacks to a second footbridge over the creek before reaching Rainbow Falls at 2.6 miles.

You'll find another footbridge just below Rainbow Falls with the waterfall back in a cove. You'll have to scramble up some rocks to get a closer view of the falls. Here LeConte Creek spills 80 feet over the descending ledges of the rock bluff and then maneuvers through a boulder field and under the trail's two nearby footbridges. If you catch the afternoon sun just right, you'll be rewarded with a rainbow reflected from the mist of the falls, which is of course how the waterfall got its name. In an especially cold winter, you will find a column of blue-white ice that is a main park attraction that time of year.

Continuing on to the summit of Mt. LeConte and LeConte Lodge, you'll cross the footbridge below the falls and continue your climb. As you gain the higher elevations, the trail switchbacks through a series of sandstone chutes lined with mountain laurel, rhododendron, and sand myrtle, blooming pink, purple, and white in May and June. At 5.4 miles the trail passes over Rocky Spur, a rock outcropping along the top of the ridge. A side trail that loops back into the main trail takes you up on the outcropping for outstanding valley views to the north.

As you continue your ascent on the main trail, you'll enter the spruce-fir zone toward the top of the mountain; the trail here becomes rocky. Then at 6.0 miles you'll reach the end of the trail at a junction with the Bullhead Trail to the right. To the left, you can climb the remaining 0.6 mile to LeConte Lodge.

Mt. LeConte, at 6593 feet the third highest peak in the national park, was an attraction in the region even before there was a park. Two points on the summit offer spectacular views—Cliff Top for sunset and Myrtle Point for sunrise. The mountain is named for Professor Joseph Le Conte, a well-known geologist in the early part of the century.

During the movement to establish the national park, the proponents thought a high country camp was needed from which visitors could explore the mountains. The Great Smoky Mountains Conservation Association enlisted a young Paul Adams, later a well-known naturalist, to establish the camp on the summit of Mt. LeConte in 1925. The camp was at first just a tent and then a cabin that Adams built near the spring that gives rise to Roaring Fork Creek. Adams guided visitors, including members of the federal Park Commission, through the mountains and forests of the Smokies. He chronicled his experiences in a journal, *Mt. LeConte*, published in 1966.

The camp was taken over in 1926 by Jack Huff and Will Ramsey. Huff eventually built a lodge with many bunk cabins and two larger cabins added for offices and dining. Today, LeConte Lodge is operated as a park concession providing meals and lodging from the end of March through mid-November; reservations must be made months in advance. Above the lodge, you'll find the Mt. LeConte shelter for backpackers.

From the summit of Mt. LeConte, you can descend by four different routes: the Alum Cave Trail to Newfound Gap Road (probably the most popular route up Mt. LeConte), the Boulevard Trail and then along the Appalachian Trail to Newfound Gap (the easiest route up the mountain), the Trillium Gap Trail to the Roaring Fork Motor Natural Trail, and the Bullhead Trail to Cherokee Orchard. Unless you return along the Rainbow Falls Trail, the Bullhead Trail is the only trail that will descend to a point near the trailhead parking area where you began this hike. It's a roundtrip of 13.5 miles.

**Mt. LeConte**

# 2 Bullhead Trail

5.9 miles one way
(LeConte Lodge 6.9 miles one way)
Difficult
Elevation gain: 4000 ft.
Cautions: Strenuous ascent, rough footing, narrow footbridge
Campsites: LeConte Lodge, Mt. LeConte Shelter
Connections: Rainbow Falls, Alum Cave, Trillium Gap,
Boulevard Trails

**Attractions**: You will have increasingly spectacular views as you climb Bullhead to LeConte Lodge.

**Trailhead**: Follow the directions in Trail #1 to the trailhead on Cherokee Orchard Road.

**Directions**: Head to your right from the parking area into the woods. Soon you'll come to an intersection of trails. The Rainbow Falls Trail is straight ahead; a connector to the Trillium Gap Trail is to the left. Turn right to get to the Bullhead Trail.

This connector trail soon joins a jeep road. Bear left with LeConte Creek on your right. You'll then cross the creek on a split-log footbridge; this is the last water you will see until you reach the summit of Mt. LeConte. At 0.4 mile, you'll find the beginning of the Bullhead Trail on the left. The connector trail you are on leads a couple of miles over to the Sugarlands Visitor Center on Newfound Gap Road.

Turn left on the Bullhead Trail, ascending through a canopy of young hemlock. As you climb through a second-growth forest, views will appear through the rhododendron and laurel lining the trail on your right.

In your ascent, the trail passes below Bullhead, a heath-covered bald on a spine running west from Mt. LeConte. You really can't see the shape from the trail, but from a distance it is said to resemble a bull's head. At about 2.5 miles you'll traverse a boulder-field bowl with an open-end view of the LeConte Creek

Valley below. You'll then switchback above Bullhead. The trail then follows the ridge, ascending toward the summit of Mt. LeConte.

You'll find outstanding views as you continue the ascent. Watch for a boulder on the left at about 3.0 miles that you can stand on to see over the heath into the valley below. On a clear day we sighted English Mountain to the northeast and Sugarland Mountain to the southwest.

From the ridge you'll climb through a mossy tunnel of rhododendron and laurel, then walk through a natural stone gateway into a conifer forest of red spruce and Frasier fir. Your steady, strenuous climb comes to an end after you round the bend below the sandstone bulwark of Balsam Point and ascend to conquer the ridge at about 6.0 miles.

As you continue along the trail you'll notice the small peak of West Point on your right. And then at 6.3 miles, you'll reach a junction with the Rainbow Falls Trail to the left and to the right a 0.6-mile climb to the summit of Mt. LeConte and LeConte Lodge. From the lodge you can connect with the Trillium Gap, Alum Cave, and Boulevard Trails.

All the roundtrip hikes up and down Mt. LeConte are over 10 miles; so unless you are in good enough condition to walk that far, you should probably plan ahead and make it an overnight trip at LeConte Lodge or a backpack with a stop at the Mt. LeConte shelter. If you intend to walk to the top and back in a day, you'll need to start in the morning and allow all day for the hike. And be sure to pack your lunch; the meals at the lodge are for overnight guests only.

**LeConte Lodge**

# ③ Trillium Gap Trail

6.5 miles one way
(Grotto Falls: 1.5 miles one way)
(Brushy Mountain: 3.2 miles one way)
Difficult
Elevation gain: 3350 ft.
Cautions: Long ascent, creek crossings
Campsites: LeConte Lodge, Mt. LeConte Shelter
Connections: Brushy Mountain, Boulevard, Alum Cave,
Rainbow Falls, Bullhead Trails

**Attractions**: One of several trails to Mt. LeConte, this route takes you by Grotto Falls and offers great views from Brushy Mountain.

**Trailhead**: Follow the directions in Trail #1 to the Rainbow Falls/Bullhead Trailhead. You can walk the 2.4 miles east from the main trail junction here to get to the beginning of the Trillium Gap Trail. But it's easier if you drive a little farther along Cherokee Orchard Road and then turn on the Roaring Fork Motor Nature Trail. At 1.7 miles from the beginning of the motor trail, you'll find the Trillium Gap/Grotto Falls parking on the left.

**Description**: From the far end of the parking area, head to the right into the woods. In 0.1 mile, you'll reach a junction with the connector trail that leads in from the Rainbow Falls parking area. Bear left to stay with the Trillium Gap Trail, which is the only horse trail to the summit of Mt. LeConte and is the trail used to transport supplies to LeConte Lodge at the top of the mountain. But rather than horses, the lodge managers have found llamas to be most efficient, so you might get to see some on the trail.

In spring you'll find a multitude of wildflowers, including trillium, as the trail makes a gentle ascent through a lowland woods. The part of the trail to Grotto Falls is an easy walk with only a 500-foot gain in elevation; the difficult rating of this trail applies to the long ascent to Mt. LeConte beyond Grotto Falls.

The trail crosses a stream on stepping stones and then circles a ravine through ferns, partridgeberry, and rhododendrons to a stand of large hemlocks. Continuing a gentle ascent, you'll cross two more streams on stepping stones until you begin paralleling the Roaring Fork below on your left. The creek is the steepest stream in the park. From its spring high on Mt. LeConte, it drops a vertical mile before joining the West Prong of the Little Pigeon River in Gatlinburg. On its way, the Roaring Fork sails 30 feet over Grotto Falls at 1.5 miles along the trail.

The waterfall got its name from the grotto that has developed behind the falls, a recess shielded by the stream of falling water. The trail actually goes behind the waterfall through this grotto. You'll have to scramble through boulders just before the falls and then take care walking behind the falls on the wet rocks.

The walk to Grotto Falls is a short day hike rewarding enough on its own. But even if you are not ascending all the way to the top of Mt. LeConte, you may want to continue on as far as Trillium Gap for the spring wildflowers and the views from Brushy Mountain.

From Grotto Falls, the trail ascends through hemlock woods, crossing one small stream, to Trillium Gap at 2.9 miles. The gap is a swag between the peaks of Mt. LeConte and the smaller Brushy Mountain. In spring, this is one of the prettiest places in the park with spring beauty scattered everywhere. The last time we were there, so many were concentrated that it seemed as if gravity had drawn the wildflowers down into the gap.

You'll find a trail intersection at the gap. To the left, you can walk 0.4 mile to the top of Brushy Mountain for fine views from the summit. Straight ahead, the Brushy Mountain Trail leads into the Greenbrier area to connect with the Porters Creek Trail in 4.5 miles. Turn right to continue on the Trillium Gap Trail.

In your ascent, you'll pass small streams that wet the trail. At 4.2 miles you'll pass through a heath bald and then a small gap and continue ascending. At 4.7 miles, the trail passes through a slide area. You'll then ascend along high ridges through red spruce and Frasier fir to the summit of Mt. LeConte and LeConte Lodge at 6.5 miles. To the left, the Boulevard Trail leads to the Appalachian Trail. To the right are the connections with the Alum Cave, Bullhead, and Rainbow Falls Trails.

**Grotto Falls**

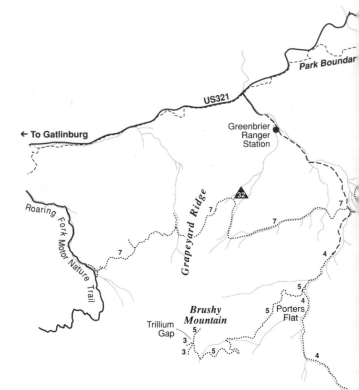

**Greenbrier Access**

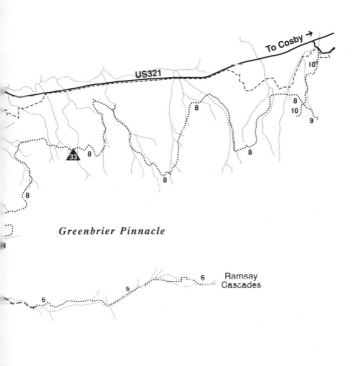

*Greenbrier Pinnacle*

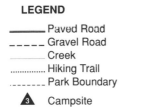

Ramsay
Cascades

## LEGEND

_____ Paved Road

_ _ _ _ Gravel Road

_____ Creek

............. Hiking Trail

_ _ _ _ _ _ Park Boundary

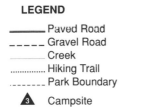 Campsite

# 4 Porters Creek Trail

3.7 miles one way
Easy
Elevation gain: 1550 ft.
Cautions: Creek crossings
Campsites: #31
Connections: Brushy Mountain Trail

**Attractions**: This trail passes the Smoky Mountains Hiking Club Cabin and presents outstanding displays of spring wildflowers.

**Trailhead**: Headed east from Gatlinburg on US321, turn south at 5.9 miles into the Greenbrier Access. The road follows along the west side of the Little Pigeon River and becomes gravel in one mile. You'll pass the Greenbrier Ranger Station on the right, and at 3.2 miles along the road, you'll come to a left turn that is the way to Ramsay Cascades. Continue straight. You'll pass a picnic area on the left and then reach the end of the road and the beginning of the Porters Creek Trail at 4 miles.

**Description**: The road actually continues on for another mile but is blocked by a gate. Begin your hike by walking up the gravel road, which gently ascends while paralleling Porters Creek, one of the tributaries of the Little Pigeon River. This is an outstanding trail for wildflowers; in March and April you'll find, even along this road section, bloodroot, trillium, may apple, trout lily, chickweed, phlox, spring beauty, toothwort.

At about 0.6 mile, you'll begin to notice moss-covered piles of stone. A small farming community once existed here; the area was called "Porters Flat" for some early settlers. At a break in a rock wall, stone steps lead up to a housesite, where you can find the foundation stones and fireplace. At 0.8 mile, you'll cross Long Branch on a wooden bridge. In spring, watch for crested dwarf iris just after the bridge.

You'll pass another set of steps on the right that lead up to a cemetery nestled under hemlocks. Just past the cemetery, the trail crosses another creek, this time without a bridge. You'll find an easier crossing just upstream.

At one mile, the road ends in a turnaround. A little to the right, you'll find the trailhead for the Brushy Mountain Trail that leads 4.5 miles to the Trillium Gap Trail. Farther to the right a side trail leads to the Smoky Mountain Hiking Club Cabin.

The Smoky Mountain Hiking Club grew out of a Knoxville YMCA group that had begun hiking the area in the early 1920s. Others wanted to join, and so the group separated from the YMCA and formally became the SMHC in 1924. The hiking club currently maintains 100 miles of the the Appalachian Trail through the park and into the Nantahala National Forest in North Carolina. In the 1930s, the club constructed the cabin on the site of the Whaley homestead. The Messer Barn you'll pass on the way to the cabin was originally the Whaley Barn, Messer having bought the homestead just before the park was established. The original Whaley frame house had been torn down, so the club used timbers that remained from two Whaley log cabins to build the hiking club cabin. When the club's special use permit expired in 1975, the park took over the cabin and now maintains it as an historic structure on the National Register of Historic Places.

Continuing on the Porters Creek Trail, a little to the left and straight ahead from the turnaround, you'll soon ascend through a mature woods of hemlock and hardwoods with rhododendron. At 1.5 miles a footbridge carries you across Porters Creek and for the remaining length, the trail follows the east side of the creek.

Beyond this creek crossing, you'll find the best wildflowers. You'll step into a spring garden of white trillium and white fringed phacelia. When we last hiked the trail in March, magnificent fields of phacelia stretched on either side with a sprinkling of trillium, geranium, dutchman's-breeches, squirrel corn, and bishop's cap. At about 2.0 miles, the trail crosses a small stream with a delicate waterfall to the left that slides down the rocks for most of its length. Beyond this waterfall, you'll find the best displays of white trillium and plaintain-leaf sedge.

The trail continues until at 3.7 miles it enters backcountry campsite #31. The trail passes beyond the campsite to soon meet the creek. At one time, the trail continued across the creek, but is now no longer maintained beyond this point.

**Hiking Club Cabin**

# ⑤ Brushy Mountain Trail

4.9 miles one way
Moderate
Elevation gain: 2500 ft.
Cautions: Stream crossings, steady climb
Campsites: none
Connections: Porters Creek, Trillium Gap Trails

**Attractions**: This trail to the summit of Brushy Mountain connects the Greenbrier and Orchard Road Access areas.

**Trailhead**: Follow the directions in Trail #4 to the beginning of the Porters Creek Trail. You must then walk a mile along that trail to the end of the old road near the Smoky Mountain Hiking Club Cabin. At the top of the road turnaround, you'll find the beginning of the Brushy Mountain Trail. This walk adds an extra mile and an additional elevation gain of 300 feet to your hike. If you want to finish your hike on the Trillium Gap Trail instead of retracing your steps, leave a car at the Grotto Falls Parking Area on the Roaring Fork Motor Nature Trail.

**Description**: The Brushy Mountain Trail first ascends gently from its junction with the Porters Creek Trail. At 0.2 mile the trail crosses a small creek. You'll soon see a stone wall on the left, a reminder that people once lived here, and cross another small creek. The trail then begins to ascend more steeply.

Through this section, you'll see frequent patches of wildflowers in spring, including violets, cinquefoil, toothwort, buttercup, trillium, chickweed, wood and rue anemones, and golden ragwort. You'll pass over another small stream that flows through rocks under the trail. At 0.4 mile you'll see on the right an old homesite marked by a collapsed chimney and wash tub. As you continue to ascend, the trail follows a creek on the right that it crosses at 0.9 mile.

At 1.0 mile, watch for large patches of wild geranium lining the trail and then on the left a pile of stone that could be another collapsed chimney. It is often difficult to tell whether a pile of stone was once a chimney or just a stack of stones picked up and brought to one place to get them out of a new cornfield.

At 1.4 miles, as you continue to climb, the trail passes large patches of yellow violets, curves left across a small stream, and then passes a gathering of yellow trillium and more violets. The trail then passes into a drier forest with rhododendron, laurel, and galax lining the trail and only a few wildflowers, although you should watch closely for the occasional trailing arbutus.

As the trail climbs, you'll come to a rock in the trail at 2.2 miles that offers a little step up to view the summit of Brushy Mountain ahead and the long northeast ridge of Mt. LeConte. You can hear Cannon Creek below, a tributary of Porters Creek. You'll pass through rhododendron and laurel and then cross a small stream. Watch for a huge poplar on the left.

At 2.7 miles, the trail crosses Trillium Branch, which flows down through moss-covered boulders to join Cannon Creek below. Around the crossing, you'll see scattered blossoms of wild hydrangea. The trail becomes lined with partridgeberry as it passes through a quiet hemlock woods. Brushy Mountain stands behind as you proceed up the trail. At 3.1 miles the trail switches back right and now the mountain looms ahead through the trees.

You'll pass more patches of the yellow violets. The last time we hiked the trail, we had to climb over occasional hemlocks that had fallen across the path. At about 3.3 miles watch for huge hemlocks growing to the right of the trail.

At 3.7 miles, you'll begin seeing fields of spring beauty in early spring that decorate the remainder of the trail. You'll also see scattered among them trout lily and squirrel corn. At 4.1 miles, you'll cross again Trillium Branch and then at 4.5 reach Trillium Gap amid thousands of spring beauty.

At the gap you can turn left on the Trillium Gap Trail to ascend to Mt. LeConte in 3.6 miles. To the right, you can reach the summit of Brushy Mountain for views of Mt. LeConte in 0.4 mile. Or you can continue straight ahead on the Trillium Gap Trail to walk by Grotto Falls and reach the Roaring Fork Motor Nature Trail in 2.8 miles. Or, after climbing to the summit of Brushy Mountain, you can return along the Brushy Mountain Trail to the Porters Creek Trailhead.

# ⑥ Ramsay Cascade Trail

4.0 miles one way
Moderate
Elevation gain: 2200 ft.
Cautions: Creek crossings, boulder passages
Campsites: None
Connections: None

**Attractions**: This popular trail ascends through a virgin forest of large trees and ends at Ramsay Cascades.

**Trailhead**: Follow the directions in Trail #4 to the left turn at 3.2 miles along the Greenbrier Road. Making the turn, you'll cross the Little Pigeon River on two bridges. The road follows along the Middle Prong of the Little Pigeon for 1.5 miles to where it is blocked; this is the trailhead for Ramsay Cascades.

**Description**: The trail begins at the end of the parking area and soon crosses the Middle Prong of the Little Pigeon River on a wooden bridge. You'll gradually ascend through large boulders and a forest of hemlock and mixed hardwood along an old roadbed with the stream on your right.

At about one mile, side streams tumble down; you'll cross a wooden bridge and continue the ascent. At 1.5 miles you'll reach a junction with the old Greenbrier Pinnacle Trail and the end of the old roadway you have been following. The trail to the top of Greenbrier Pinnacle is no longer maintained by the park and is gradually becoming overgrown as the forest reclaims the path. A firetower once stood atop the pinnacle, but no longer. The use of lookout towers for fire control ended in 1968 because the forest had recovered enough that the fire danger was less than it had been. In addition, a new philosophy of containing fires rather than necessarily extinguishing them had been adopted. Fire watch is now performed by occasional airplane flights over the park and staff patrols.

**Crossing Ramsay Prong**

The Ramsay Cascade Trail continues from the end of the old roadway as a footpath. Ramsay Prong, a tributary of the Middle Prong, flows past on the right. At about 2.0 miles, the trail opens into a canyon with the creek flowing over boulders and swirling below. A log footbridge takes you across the rushing stream.

You'll continue your climb, now through one of the largest pockets of virgin forest in the Smokies. The trees include hemlock, poplar, black cherry, silverbell, yellow and sweet birch, and cucumber magnolia, which blooms large yellowish flowers in late April and early May. At one point you'll pass between massive poplars, some of the largest trees in the park.

The trail soon skirts the creek, which is now on the left, and at 3.0 miles reaches another log footbridge across the stream. Just before the bridge, an opening provides a good opportunity to take a photograph of your hiking partners as they cross the bridge.

You'll rockhop the stream a couple of times. The trail then swings away from Ramsay Prong for a time and then back, makes a side-stream crossing, and then follows along the creek. The trail narrows as it climbs through boulder passages to eventually emerge at Ramsay Cascades, a 90-foot-high spillway in which the Ramsay Prong falls as double streams that converge halfway down to cascade into the pool below. Ramsay Cascades and Ramsay Prong get their name from the Ramsays who in the mid-1800s had a hunting camp of lean-tos in the area. Ramsay Cascades is the tallest waterfall in the park that can be reached by trail. Mill Creek Falls, off-trail in the western part of the park, is reported to be the tallest.

Unfortunately, Ramsay Cascades is a popular destination; so while you may have solitude much of the time while walking the trail, you'll probably have to take your turn standing at the base of the falls. Even when we were there on a late fall day that was damp and cool, a group of a half dozen people occupied the area at the base of the cascades and others arrived before we left.

There are no trail connections from this point. You must retrace your steps to the beginning of the trail.

**Ramsay Cascades**

# 7 Grapeyard Ridge Trail

7.6 miles one way
Moderate
Elevation change: 1000 ft.
Cautions: Numerous stream crossings
Campsites: #32
Connections: Old Settlers, Big Dudley Trails

**Attractions**: Wildflowers are abundant on this trail that leads past old homesites and along Injun Creek where you'll find the remains of an old steam engine.

**Trailhead**: Follow the directions in Trail #4 to just before the turn to Ramsay Cascades; the Grapeyard Ridge Trail begins on the right side of the road. You'll find parking for a couple of vehicles on the left. You can link up with the Old Settlers Trail at this junction by turning down the road to Ramsay Cascades. If you plan on walking all the way to the Roaring Fork Motor Nature Trail on the Grapeyard Ridge Trail, you can have a car pick you up at the small parking area at guidepost #8, 0.7 mile past the Grotto Falls turnout.

**Description**: The Grapeyard Ridge Trail ascends from the road into a mixed rhododendron, laurel, hemlock, and hardwood forest. Notice the rock wall on the right. The trail follows what was probably an old roadbed, and you'll see several old homesites and rock walls along the way. Just past the rock wall, you'll see another old roadway taking off to the right, but stay straight.

Still climbing, the trail passes another old roadway on the left and at 0.2 mile connects with a more obvious old road and turns right. You'll level off and then climb again to top the ridge at 0.5 mile. Watch for an old homesite on the right marked by a pile of stones. The trail then descends into a hollow. At 0.7 mile an old cornfield lies on the left, now being reclaimed by the forest. You'll cross a small stream at 0.8 mile. Watch for another homesite on the right.

You'll cross a small creek at 0.9 mile and soon see another old homesite on the left as you ascend through rhododendron. At about 1.3 miles, the trail crosses Rhododendron Creek; there's a log you can use to get over. The next section of trail follows along Rhododendron Creek upstream, intertwining with the creek and its tributaries as you make your way up the valley that was once cleared for farming; you'll have several creek crossings where you rockhop to get across. In spring, you'll find in the bottomland carpets of wildflowers, including spring beauty, mayapple, trillium, toothwort, chickweed, and rue anemone.

At about 2.2 miles, the trail begins an ascent of James Ridge and passes over the ridge at James Gap at 2.7 miles. In the gap, there appears to have been another homesite up to the right. The trail then drops off the ridge to cross Injun Creek. Just below the crossing you'll find in the creek an old steam engine that was probably used in log skidding during the lumbering operations in the area in the early part of the century. It appears the engine rolled over into the creek and was just left where it lay. Interesting that the creek is named "Injun," as in "Indian," rather than "Engine."

The trail continues to descend, with Injun Creek stairstepping down the mountain on your right. At 3.2 miles, you'll reach the side trail on the right that leads 100 yards to campsite #32 on Injun Creek. The side trail follows an old roadbed that continues past the campsite in the direction of the Greenbrier Ranger Station.

Continue straight past this side trail. You'll cross a small stream and then begin the climb up Grapeyard Ridge. At 3.4 miles, you'll cross another small stream and keep climbing through a switchback left and later a switchback right. You'll reach a pass at 3.8 miles and then wind along the slope of the ridge to then climb more gradually, finally topping the ridge at 4.2 miles. This last section of trail is great for wildflowers in spring; the slopes are clothed in bloodroot, rue anemone, spring beauty, trout lily, wood anemone, and toothwort.

After passing over the ridge, you'll descend and soon switchback left. At 4.8 miles, the trail crosses Dudley Creek amid old stone walls and wildflowers. To the left, you'll see where a bridge once crossed the stream; the stone footings remain. Follow the old roadbed covered in periwinkle to the right. At 4.9 miles,

**Injun Creek**

you'll reach a junction with the Big Dudley Trail that leads 2.5 miles to the right to the Smoky Mountain Riding Stables on US321. Turn left to stay on the Grapeyard Ridge Trail. You'll ascend a ridge running north from Mt. Winnesoka. You'll top the ridge at 6.1 miles and descend to a fork in the trail. The right fork circles around to the stables on US321 in 2 miles. You should take the left fork.

At 6.3 miles the trail crosses a stream thick with wildflowers, watch for large patches of wild geranium a little farther. At 6.5 miles the trail crosses another small stream where the slope above is covered in trout lily. The trail then passes over a small ridge and descends steeply. You'll switchback left and cross a small stream pouring through a bowl of boulders. Continue descending and you'll see white erect trillium on the slopes until a junction at 7.5 miles. To the right the trail leads down to the motor nature trail to cross the loop and arrive at Cherokee Orchard in 4 miles. But turn left at this junction. You'll ascend and then descend to a fording of a branch of Roaring Fork Creek. The trail then ascends and descends to a second branch crossing right beside the motor nature trail. When you emerge on the road, you'll be about 0.1 mile below the parking area at guidepost #8.

# ⑧ Old Settlers Trail

15.9 miles one way
Moderate
Elevation gain: 1200 ft.
Cautions: Numerous creek crossings
Connections: Maddron Bald, Gabes Mountain,
Grapeyard Ridge Trails

**Attractions**: Although this is a long trail, it is a fairly moderate lowland path that has good displays of wildflowers in spring and frequent remains of old settlements.

**Trailhead**: Follow the directions in Trail #4 past the trailhead for the Grapeyard Ridge Trail on the right and turn left on the road to Ramsay Cascades. In 0.1 mile after crossing the second bridge, you'll find parking and the Old Settlers Trailhead on the left. If you want to do a car shuttle at the other end, follow the directions in Trail #10 to the Maddron Bald Trailhead. The total walking distance will be 17.1 miles.

**Description**: From the trailhead, the Old Settlers Trail begins in a bottomland of hemlock and hardwood, paralleling a small stream on the right. You can still hear the Little Pigeon River on your left. Watch for patches of crested dwarf iris along the trail in spring.

At 0.3 mile, you'll cross Bird Branch and then begin an ascent of a ridge. The trail passes a rock overhang on the right and then crosses a small creek. You'll then top the rise and descend to a bottomland where you'll cross several small streams amid large patches of wild geranium, crested dwarf iris, foam flower, and phlox that bloom in spring. The trail also passes old rock walls, your first sign of the old settlements that were frequent along these lowlands in the first part of the century before the park was created.

At 1.2 miles you'll cross Little Bird Branch and then ascend while paralleling the branch. The trail then ascends more steeply, eventually affording views to the east of Greenbrier Pinnacle with its bare rock walls towering over the valley. When you top the ridge at 1.9 miles, you'll curve right and, after crossing the ridge, descend the other side.

You'll eventually reach a crossing of Snakefeeder Branch at 2.5 miles; watch for a 6-foot waterfall upstream. The trail then ascends from the branch to the top of a ridge at 2.9 miles that affords views through the trees to the mountain range deeper in the park. As the trail descends the other side of the ridge, it crosses a small branch of Soak Ash Creek at 3.5 miles and then crosses the main stem of the creek twice and then a third time at an old homesite on the left with half a chimney still standing amid scattered rock.

The trail continues to descend along Soak Ash Creek until you reach an open lowland where you'll cross several small streams. You'll then ascend along what becomes an old road to a junction at 4.7 miles. An unmaintained path continues straight on the old roadbed. Turn right to stay on the Old Settlers Trail and ascend along an old roadway; watch for rock walls. You'll cross Timothy Creek at 5.7 miles and ascend to pass an old homesite; notice on the right the small outbuilding that was probably either a chicken coop or hog pen. You'll reach campsite #33 at 6.7 miles with an old chimney standing in its midst.

From the campsite, the trail soon drops to a crossing of Redwine Creek and then ascends steeply. The trail climbs along a drier slope of pine and laurel and reaches the top of the ridge at 7.4 miles. You'll then descend, joining Ramsey Creek. As the trail continues to descend you'll pass old homesites and cross the creek five times. At the last crossing at 8.1 miles, watch for a small waterfall upstream.

As you continue to descend with Ramsey Creek now on your left, you'll notice many wild geranium in spring at the creek's edge. At 8.3 miles, the trail turns away from the creek on an old roadbed. You'll pass several rock walls and reach a junction at 8.9 miles. An unmaintained path straight ahead joins Noisy Creek and follows it out to US321. Turn right on another old roadbed to stay on the Old Settlers Trail, which now parallels Noisy Creek upstream. At 9.3 miles, the trail turns left to cross Noisy Creek at an old ford.

**Old Settler's Housesite**

The trail continues upstream along the creek, passing rock walls and old homesites marked by rock piles that are either collapsed chimneys or piles of rock left from cleared fields. At a homesite where yuccas still grow, the trail crosses Noisy Creek again. And then at 9.6 miles, you'll cross the creek again.

You'll pass through an open area once farmed and then begin an ascent into a wooded area. At 10.1 miles the trail crosses Tumbling Branch and continues to ascend with some ups and downs and then more steeply. The forest is now made up of more mature trees, including some large hemlocks. This ridge slope was apparently not settled. As you near the top of the ridge, you'll see the prone hulks of old chestnut trees that long ago succumbed to the chestnut blight.

You'll top the ridge at 10.9 miles, the highest point on the Old Settlers Trail. The trail then descends the other side to a crossing of Texas Creek. You'll then continue to descend along the creek, passing old homesites and crossing small streams. Watch for patches of wild geranium and crested dwarf iris.

At 11.8 miles after descending more steeply, you'll encounter an old homesite on the right with a chimney still standing intact. This is the best preserved chimney on the Old Settlers Trail. Past the homesite, the trail still descends, following an old roadbed to a right turn on another old roadbed at 12.0 miles.

The trail then descends to a bottomland, where you'll cross a small stream and curve right. You'll then follow a small water course upstream, finally crossing it and curving left to encounter rock walls. Eventually there are rock walls on both sides of the trail, which follows an old country lane. The wall on the left is about 5 feet high and 2 feet thick. The trail runs right into Webb Creek at 12.8 miles. On the other side you'll find rock foundations of an old house.

After the crossing, the trail turns right, following the creek upstream. You'll pass numerous rock walls and collapsed chimneys. At 13.0 miles, the trail passes right through a rock wall. As you continue to ascend, you'll step over a small creek making its way to join Webb Creek. At 13.8 miles the trail makes a left turn away from Webb Creek. You'll see the remains of a log cabin on the right and leftover daylilies.

You'll then descend to a crossing of the small creek you crossed earlier. The trail then passes over a small rise and then begins a climb, passing through thick rhododendron and laurel to reach the ridgeline of Snag Mountain. To the right you'll see Greenbrier Pinnacle through the trees.

The trail rounds a point at 14.2 miles and begins a descent You'll enter a cove as you descend, crossing a small creek and passing a homesite with jonquils blooming in spring. At 14.4 miles, you'll cross the creek again and enter a bottomland while paralleling the creek downstream. At 15.0 miles watch for a 3-foot-high rock wall on the right.

You'll then drop to a crossing of Dunn Creek. The trail ascends to an old homesite with collapsed chimney and wall on the right and then descends to a crossing of Indian Camp Creek at 15.4 miles. This is a major crossing, but when we hiked the trail last, a fallen tree lay across the creek to help us with the crossing; it will probably still be there when you make the hike.

Climbing from the creek, you'll pass another old homesite and then drop to a crossing of Maddron Creek at 15.6 miles. After climbing from this crossing, you'll follow an old road through remains of old settlements, piles of rock from cleared fields and collapsed chimneys. You'll then ascend to the end of the trail at a junction with the Maddron Bald Trail, which leads 6.0 miles to the right to the top of Maddron Bald. Straight ahead you can connect with the Gabes Mountain Trail that leads 6.6 miles to the Cosby area. To the left the Maddron Bald Trail leads 1.2 miles out to Laurel Spring Road off US321.

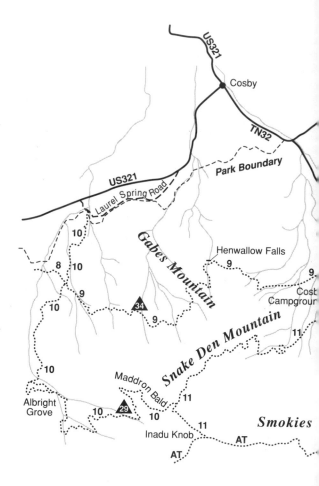

**Cosby Access**

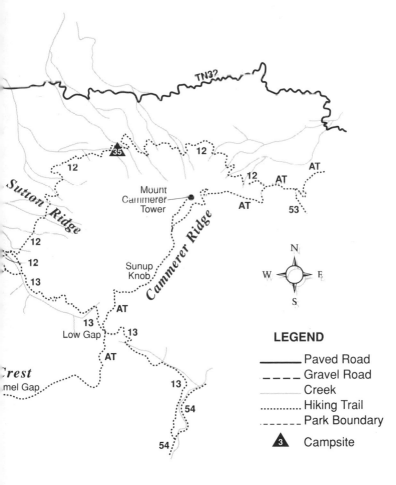

TN32

35

12

12

Mount
Cammerer
Tower

Sutton Ridge

Cammerer Ridge

12

12

13

Sunup
Knob

AT

13

13

Low Gap

AT

rest

mel Gap

12

AT

AT

AT

53

13

54

54

N
W   E
S

**LEGEND**

─────── Paved Road

─ ─ ─ Gravel Road

──────── Creek

·············· Hiking Trail

─ ─ ─ ─ Park Boundary

▲ 3   Campsite

# ⑨ Gabes Mountain Trail

6.6 miles one way
(Henwallow Falls 2.1 miles one way)
Moderate
Elevation gain: 1300 ft.
Cautions: Stream crossings
Campsites: #34
Connections: Maddron Bald, Old Settlers Trails

**Attractions**: This trail passes by Henwallow Falls and through mature forest and is the first leg of one of the best backpacking loops in the park.

**Trailhead**: To get to the Cosby Access, take TN32 southwest from Cosby, which can be reached by taking US321 east from Gatlinburg or by taking the Foothills Parkway west from I-40. At 1.2 miles south of Cosby, a right turn takes you into Cosby Cove. (If you were to continue straight on TN32 for about 10 miles, you would reach the Big Creek Access.) In about 2 miles after making the turn, you'll reach the Cosby picnic area with parking for day hiking. If you are backpacking, you'll need to proceed ahead to the backpacking parking area just past the registration hut.

**Description**: From the picnic parking area walk a hundred yards back along the road in the direction from which you entered to the trailhead on the left and a sign for the Gabes Mountain Trail. The trail ascends from the road gradually for a quarter mile to a fork with the main trail to the right and a side trail to the Cosby Campground to the left.

Staying to the right, you'll gradually ascend through mixed hardwoods and hemlocks and cross Rock Creek on a footbridge. On its way, the trail crosses several tributaries of Crying Creek, sometimes on footbridges but at other times across stepping stones. At 1.0 mile you'll encounter a left turn. The old route of the Gabes Mountain Trail is to the right, which once came out on the road closer to the Cosby Access entrance.

Turn left, and from this junction the trail ascends along the flank of Gabes Mountain past rock outcrops at 1.5 miles and then levels off to a side trail on the right to Henwallow Falls at 2.1 miles. This side trail descends steeply through switchbacks to the base of the 40-foot waterfall that fans out as it cascades down to where you stand. The falls and Henwallow Creek probably got their names from someone seeing nearby a ruffed grouse wallowing in dust, a common practice of this "wood hen."

From this side trail, the main trail continues straight ahead and passes over the Lower Falling Branch of Henwallow Creek above the waterfall. The trail then switches back and climbs gradually, eventually recrossing the creek twice and climbing through a mountain gap. You'll then enter a remnant virgin forest of huge hemlocks and poplars. This quiet, partridgeberry-lined section of the trail is well worth the walk to get there. So if you intend to walk just part of the trail and then backtrack to the Cosby parking area, you may want to walk as far as 3.0 to 3.5 miles to see the first of these trees.

As the trail continues through these large trees, it undulates along the side of the mountain, crossing Gabes Creek. At about 4.3 miles, you'll top a ridge in a stand of massive hemlocks and then drop into Sugar Cove. At 4.8 miles, the trail crosses Greenbrier Creek; you'll find backcountry campsite #34 on the other side.

From the campsite, the trail ascends to a small pass at 5.0 miles and then descends along Cole Creek. The trail eventually emerges from the forest to a junction with the Maddron Bald Trail, which at this point is an old gravel road. Immediately across the road is the east end of the Old Settlers Trail. The Maddron Bald Trail to the right takes you 1.2 miles to the Laurel Spring Road off US321, which is convenient for doing a car shuttle back to Cosby.

The Gabes Mountain Trail, the Maddron Bald Trail to the left, and the Snake Den Ridge Trail as the return to Cosby create a 17.2-mile loop that is one of the best backpacking trips in the park. The loop takes you by Henwallow Falls, through virgin timber that includes the Albright Grove, and up and over Maddron Bald before descending back to the parking area at Cosby.

**Henwallow Falls**

# 10 Maddron Bald Trail

7.2 miles one way
(Albright Grove, 3.0 miles one way)
Difficult
Elevation gain: 3500 feet
Cautions: Creek crossings, steep ascent near the top
Campsites: #29
Connections: Gabes Mountain, Old Settlers,
Snake Den Ridge Trails

**Attractions**: This trail ascends to a heath bald with several good views and along the way takes you by the Albright Grove Nature Trail that contains the park's best stand of virgin forest.

**Trailhead**: On US321 between Cosby and Gatlinburg, 15 miles east of Gatlinburg, turn south on Laurel Spring Road, a small gravel road on the west side of the Yogi Bear Jellystone Park Camp Resort. At 0.2 mile along this road, you'll encounter a gravel road on the right that is blocked by a gate. This is the beginning of the trail.

**Description**: The trail ascends at first gradually and then more steeply along the gravel road for 1.2 miles to the junction of the Gabes Mountain Trail to the left and the Old Settlers Trail to the right. In spring watch for frequent showy orchis in bloom, a relatively rare orchid that seems to frequent old roadsides in the Smokies.

This first stretch of trail, which once was called the "Indian Camp Creek Trail" but is now part of the Maddron Bald Trail, passes through old farmland now covered in second-growth timber. About a half mile from the beginning of the trail, you'll pass the Willis Baxter Cabin on the right, built in 1889.

From the intersection with the Old Settlers Trail and Gabes Mountain Trail, the Maddron Bald Trail continues straight ahead, still following the gravel road, ascending most of the way. You'll reach the end of the road at a turnaround at 2.3 miles. The trail

**Willis Baxter Cabin**

then enters the forest and ascends steadily and crosses Indian Camp Creek on a new footbridge.

At 3.2 miles you'll reach the Albright Grove Nature Trail on the right. The 0.7-mile nature trail loops south and east to rejoin the Maddron Bald Trail at about 0.2 mile farther up the trail. Albright Grove, named for Horace M. Albright, director of the National Park Service 1929-1933 and one of the proponents for establishing the Great Smoky Mountains National Park, is probably the best stand of virgin forest in the park. You'll find here the largest known specimen of the Tennessee State Tree, the tulip poplar, 135 feet high and 25 feet 3 inches in circumference. Tulip poplars are the largest living things in the park.

From the nature trail, the main trail climbs continuously. You'll have several crossings of both Indian Camp and Copperhead Creeks. At 5.0 miles, a short path to a rock outcropping to the left leads to a point from which you can see Maddron Bald to the northeast and the Indian Camp Creek Valley below.

At about 5.7 miles, the trail leads across Otter Creek to backcountry campsite #29. This campsite is frequented by bears; you'll find a cable strung between trees that should be used to hang your food if you're spending the night. When we spent the night here, we saw no sign of bears.

From the campsite, the trail climbs steeply, finally breaking out on Maddron Bald at around 6 miles. This is one of the heath balds—mountain ridges covered in laurel, rhododendron, and occasional blueberry, huckleberry, azalea, and sand myrtle. It is still not fully understood why heath balds occur, but it probably has to do with a combination of the dry rocky terrain, lightning fires, and the suppression of tree growth by the shrubs once they get established. Heath balds are sometimes called "laurel slicks" because of the wet appearance of the shiny laurel leaves. The heath balds were also called "hells" by the early settlers because the thickets were so difficult to walk through. You'll find the trail keeps you from having to plow through the tangled growth of the heath. With occasional rock outcrops along the trail, you'll be able to see above the heath for views of the surrounding valleys.

At 7.2 miles, the trail intersects with the Snake Den Ridge Trail. To the left, you can reach the Cosby Campground in 4.6 miles. To the right, you'll find the Appalachian Trail in 0.7 mile.

# 11 Snake Den Ridge Trail

5.3 miles one way
Moderate
Elevation gain: 3600 feet
Cautions: Creek crossings, long ascent
Campsites: Cosby Campground
Connections: Low Gap, Maddron Bald, Appalachian Trails

**Attractions**: This trail shows you what the Smokies are famous for, a mountain walk lined with forest, ferns, and rhododendrons.

**Trailhead**: Follow the directions in Trail #9 to the Cosby parking area and proceed into the campground to the southwest corner were you'll find a gated gravel road at campsite B55.

**Description**: Walk up the gravel road. At about 0.2 mile, a horse trail joins from the left that is a connector with the Low Gap Trail. Along the road you'll walk through second-growth deciduous forest, and in the fall, the woods are draped in brilliant reds and yellows and gold. The road ends at 0.8 mile.

Continue on the trail from the end of the road, gradually ascending to cross Rock Creek on a footbridge at 1.0 mile. The trail then climbs along Inadu Creek on the right to cross at 2.0 miles. "Inadu" means "snake" in Cherokee and comes from the snake dens on the mountain. We saw no snakes.

The trail climbs up the ridge of Snake Den Mountain through a series of switchbacks. At 2.4 miles, an overlook provides a view of Cosby Cove. The trail alternately passes over dry ridges of pine and laurel and then through hemlock forests with rhododendron and ferns lining the path. At 4.3 miles the trail emerges onto a heath bald where the path becomes rocky. At 4.6 miles you'll encounter the junction with the Maddron Bald Trail on the right that drops steeply all the way to US321 in 7.2 miles.

Continuing straight ahead, the Snake Den Ridge Trail passes spruce and fir as it gains the crest of the mountain range at 5.3 miles where it joins the Appalachian Trail at Inadu Knob.

# 12 Lower Mount Cammerer Trail

7.4 miles one way
(Mt. Cammerer firetower 10.3 miles one way)
Difficult
Elevation gain: 2600 ft. to fire tower
Cautions: Overgrown
Campsites: Cosby Campground, #35
Connections: Appalachian, Low Gap Trails

**Attractions**: This trail is part of a long backpack loop that takes you by the Mt. Cammerer firetower.

**Trailhead**: Follow the directions in Trail #9 into Cosby. You can begin this trail near campsite B100 in the campground, but there is limited parking at this trailhead and the campground is closed in winter, so you may need to park at the backpackers' parking area near the registration hut. A trail there leads right to connect with the Lower Mt. Cammerer Trail, adding 0.4 mile to your hike.

**Description**: From the trailhead in the campground, walk around the gate and up the gravel road. At 0.1 mile the road fords Cosby Creek, but you can take the footbridge to the right. You'll then pass on the left the access trail from the parking area near the registration hut. You'll then enter the Cosby Stables area where a connector trail to the right leads to the Low Gap Trail.

Continue straight through the horse area up the gravel road, which begins a gradual ascent. At 0.3 mile, the road crosses a small stream. You'll then walk over a hill and descend to where a stream flows under the road. Uphill again, you'll reach a spring on the right that is walled in by rocks. Another stream passes under the road, and then at 0.6 mile the trail turns to the right on a footpath while the road ahead circles back to the stables.

The trail now ascends through hardwood and rhododendron to a rockhop crossing of a creek at 0.9 mile that flows down to Toms Creek you'll hear on your left. The trail then descends to cross this main creek on a footbridge at 1.0 mile. You'll then climb to top Sutton Ridge at 1.2 miles. Here a side trail to the right climbs 200 yards to a view over Cosby Valley.

The trail then descends the other side of Sutton Ridge to where a long slender stream cascades down innumerable steps to pass under the trail at 1.8 miles. You'll have more downhill, and then up and level to rockhop a stream at 2.1 miles. The trail then ascends with streams passing under the trail and stretches that can get overgrown with stinging nettle that hurries you along. At 2.9 miles a large poplar tree stands on the right. At 3.5 miles, you'll rockhop Gilliland Creek and then ascend steeply to campsite #35 at 3.6 miles.

The trail continues straight, rounds a point, and ascends to another rockhop stream crossing at 3.9 miles. As you continue up the moderate ascent of Cammerer Ridge, you'll cross several small streams and wade through overgrown sections. At 6.7 miles watch for large trees, first maple, then oaks and poplars.

At 7.4 miles, the Lower Mt. Cammerer Trail ends at a junction with the Appalachian Trail at the crest of the Smokies. To the left, the AT leads 2.9 miles to the park boundary at Davenport Gap. Turn right to ascend toward the summit of Mt. Cammerer, named for Arno B. Cammerer, director of the National Park Service 1933-1940 and supporter of the establishment of the park; earlier as associate director, Cammerer determined the boundaries of the then-proposed park.

You'll ascend along the AT through a hardwood forest. The trail passes a rock outcropping that gives a view to the northeast and ascends into the spruce-fir zone. At 2.3 miles along the AT, you'll reach a gap where the Mt. Cammerer Trail leads right 0.6 mile out to the Mt. Cammerer firetower perched atop a rock outcropping known locally as "White Rocks," which gives one of the best views in the park. The firetower, constructed in the late 1930s by the CCC is a stone and wood construction that because of its unique character has been listed on the National Register; the Appalachian Trail Club has established a fund to restore the structure, which is now in disrepair.

From the Mt. Cammerer Trail, you can continue west on the AT to connect with the Low Gap Trail to make a loop back to the Cosby Campground, a total of 15.5 miles, including the walk up to the firetower and back.

**Mt. Cammerer Tower**

# 13 Low Gap Trail

5.0 miles one way
(Mt. Cammerer firetower 5.2 miles one way)
Moderate
Elevation gain: 2600 ft. to firetower
Cautions: Creek crossings, steep ascent
Campsites: Cosby Campground
Connections: Snake Den Ridge, Lower Mt. Cammerer,
Appalachian, Big Creek Trails

**Attractions**: This trail provides a shorter route to the Mt. Cammerer firetower and forms a loop hike with the Appalachian Trail and the Lower Mt. Cammerer Trail.

**Trailhead**: Follow the directions in Trail #12 to the Lower Mt. Cammerer Trailhead. Just before campsite B100, you'll see also the trailhead for the Low Gap Trail. If there is no parking or if the campground is closed, you must park outside the campground and take the connector to the Lower Mt. Cammerer Trail.

**Description**: Walk around the gate and up the gravel road. You'll soon pass by a water tank for the campground on the right and then an old water treatment structure on the left. At 0.2 mile you'll reach a connector trail to the right that links the Low Gap Trail with the Snake Den Ridge Trail. Continue up the road until at 0.3 mile you reach a turnaround at the end of the road.

Now follow a footpath into the woods. At 0.4 mile, you'll cross Cosby Creek on a footbridge and then encounter a trail to the left. This is the connector that leads 0.4 mile to intersect with the Lower Mt. Cammerer Trail at the Cosby horse stables and then another 0.4 mile to the backpackers' parking area. Continue straight here up the Low Gap Trail.

The trail ascends up Cosby Creek, with a ravine separating the trail from the creek on your right. At 0.6 mile, you'll curve left to part from Cosby Creek and pass over small streams and enter a hemlock wood. The trail curves left at 0.9 mile and continues to ascend through large hemlocks and poplars. Watch for a large poplar that leans over but then bends and stretches straight up for the light above the canopy.

The trail ascends steeply as you pass more large trees and skirt Cosby Creek again. At 1.1 miles the trail switchbacks right; you'll then pass between two large hemlocks, the one on the left a little uphill. You'll brush Cosby Creek again as the trail curves to the left and ascend steeply along a rocky path. At 1.2 miles, you'll switchback right, pass a huge oak tree, and ascend through a cove where a stream passes under the trail at 1.5 miles.

Still ascending, watch for a large double oak to the left of the trail at 2.0 miles. At 2.1 miles, the trail crosses Cosby Creek, which at this elevation is a shallow stream. You'll ascend steeply from the creek crossing to round two rocky points and reach Low Gap at 2.5 miles and an intersection with the Appalachian Trail.

It was here that we stopped for a snack. But we were interrupted when a black bear came wandering up the trail sniffing the air. He saw us and rose on his hind legs to get a better view and then lowered himself back to the ground. Advancing on us in a meandering way, he watched us out the corner of his eye, wondering what goodies we had to eat. He was a small bear, easily intimidated, but we gathered up our things and left; after all, it is his home.

From Low Gap, the Low Gap Trail leads 2.5 miles down the North Carolina side of the mountains to connect with the Big Creek Trail out of the Big Creek Access. The AT from the gap, leads right 2.4 miles past the Cosby Knob Shelter and on to Camel Gap. Turn left on the AT to head for Mt. Cammerer.

You'll ascend from Low Gap into the spruce-fir zone as the trail makes its way up the ridge. You'll skirt north around Sunup Knob and then descend to a gap and the junction with the Mt. Cammerer Trail at 2.1 miles along the AT. It's then 0.6 mile out to the Mt. Cammerer firetower and views in all directions.

From this junction with the Mt. Cammerer Trail you can return along the same route to the Cosby Campground, or you can continue down the AT to the junction with the Lower Mt. Cammerer Trail and return along that trail for a 15.5-mile loop back to the campground.

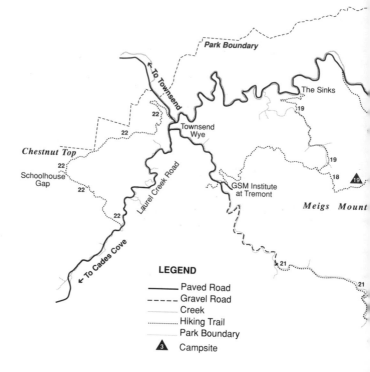

**Little River Road and Townsend Wye Access**

84

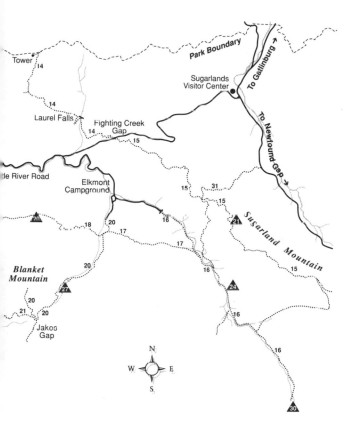

Tower

14

14

Laurel Falls

14

Fighting Creek
Gap

15

le River Road

Elkmont
Campground

15  31

15

18      20

20

17

17

16

20

16

15

*Blanket
Mountain*

16

20

21    20

Jakes
Gap

16

N

W       E

S

Park Boundary

Sugarlands
Visitor Center

To Gatlinburg

To Newfound Gap

Sugarland Mountain

# 14 Laurel Falls Trail

4.0 miles one way
(Laurel Falls 1.3 miles one way)
Moderate
Elevation gain: 1800 ft.
Cautions: Waterfall crossing
Campsites: None
Connections: Sugarland Mountain, Little Greenbrier,
Cove Mountain Trails

**Attractions**: After passing Laurel Falls on this trail, you'll ascend through virgin forest to the firetower on Cove Mountain.

**Trailhead**: From the Sugarlands Visitor Center and Park Headquarters on Newfound Gap Road, head west on Little River Road and drive 3.7 miles to the parking area at Fighting Creek Gap.

**Description**: On the south side of the road you'll find the trailhead for the Sugarland Mountain Trail that ascends 12.1 miles along the ridge of Sugarland Mountain to the Appalachian Trail running along the main ridgecrest in the park. The Laurel Falls Trail begins on the north side of the road. Laurel Falls is a popular destination and the trail is a designated nature trail, and so this first section has been paved to prevent erosion by the multitudes walking to see the falls.

At 1.3 miles, Laurel Branch spills down from the highlands to cross the trail at Laurel Falls. The 75-foot waterfall is especially interesting because it is a two-step waterfall, with the trail crossing a ledge between the upper and lower falls. You'll have to hop across boulders to get across. The water from the falls passes under you, spills down the second falls to your left, and proceeds down the narrow canyon.

Beyond the falls, the trail is no longer paved, and along this stretch you'll find more solitude. The trail ascends gradually through rhododendron and laurel and a couple of switchbacks until at 2.0 miles you'll enter a forest of giant tulip poplar and

86

hemlock standing guard along the trail. Beyond this poplar/ hemlock woods, you'll also find old-growth oaks and red maple with interspersed silverbell, a tree that has white bell-shaped flowers in spring.

At 3.1 miles the trail reaches a junction with the Little Greenbrier Trail to the left, which runs for 4.3 miles to Wear Cove Gap on the road headed north from the Metcalf Bottoms picnic area on Little River Road to Wear Cove. At the end of the Little Greenbrier Trail, you would turn left down the road a short distance to pickup the Roundtop Trail, which then leads 7.6 miles farther west to the Townsend Wye.

Keep straight at this junction with the Little Greenbrier Trail, and you'll follow Chinquapin Ridge to the crest of Cove Mountain at 4.0 miles. You'll find a junction with the Cove Mountain Trail that to the right leads 8.6 miles east to the park headquarters and the Sugarlands Visitor Center.

To the left in a little over a hundred yards you'll find a park fire lookout tower. From here, to the northwest you'll look across Wear Cove to Chilhowee Mountain outside the park where the Foothills Parkway runs along the ridge. To the southeast, you'll see deep into the park where the main crest of the Smokies shapes the skyline. But we do not recommend climbing the old firetower steps.

The Cove Mountain lookout tower is one of three that remain in the park, in addition to the historic structure on Mt. Cammerer. The other two are atop Mount Sterling and the Shuckstack on the North Carolina side of the mountains. Once there were also firetowers on Spruce Mountain, Greenbrier Pinnacle, High Rocks, Bunker Hill, Rich Mountain, and Blanket Mountain.

# 15 Sugarland Mountain Trail

12.1 miles one way
(Mt. LeConte Overlook 2.3 miles one way)
Moderate
Elevation Gain: 3500 ft.
Cautions: Long ascents
Campsites: #21, Mt. Collins Shelter
Connections: Laurel Falls, Huskey Gap, Rough Creek,
Appalachian Trails

**Attractions**: This ascending trail connects Little River Road with the Smokies crest, passing a good view of Mt. LeConte.

**Trailhead**: Follow the directions in Trail #14 to the Laurel Falls parking on Little River Road. To do a shuttle, you'll need to leave a car at the parking area for the Fork Ridge Trail 3.6 miles along Clingmans Dome Road from its beginning at Newfound Gap.

**Description**: From the road, the Laurel Falls Trail leads north to Laurel Falls and Cove Mountain. On the south side of the road, the Sugarland Mountain Trail begins a climb of the ridge of Sugarland Mountain. The trail almost immediately switches left.

You'll first climb through a pine-hemlock woods, but the trail soon turns right into a hardwood forest. You'll climb steeply and cross the upper reaches of a ravine and a small stream and then at 0.2 mile cross another small stream. At 0.6 mile the trail levels off on a drier pine-laurel ridge. You'll pass through a beech gap and then begin a gradual climb.

At 0.7 mile, the trail makes a long descent to Mids Gap at 1.2 miles, thick with rhododendron. You'll see here the junction of old trails no longer maintained. Keep straight as the trail begins another ascent. To your right is the deep cove of Mids Branch. At 1.9 miles, you'll swing around the head of a ravine and then once again reach a dry ridge of pine and laurel. The trail follows the ridge and at 2.3 miles reaches a grand open view of the Sugarland Valley sweeping up to Mt. LeConte.

**View of Sugarland Valley**

From the view, the trail makes a gradual climb, passing through several small gaps, reaching Huskey Gap and the intersection of the Huskey Gap Trail at 3.1 miles. To the left, the Huskey Gap Trail leads 2.0 miles down to the Newfound Gap Road. To the right, it leads 2.1 miles to connect with the Little River Road that heads back into Elkmont. Either of these routes makes a good dayhike if you have a car waiting for you at the end.

The Sugarland Mountain Trail continues straight. You'll make a gradual climb along a drier south-facing slope. At 3.2 miles, the trail sweeps right through another small gap and then enters a hardwood forest. Watch for the many thick patches of galax along the trail; in winter the galax leaves are a dark ruby red.

At 4.1 miles you'll reach campsite #21 beside a small stream. The trail crosses the stream and continues its ascent of Sugarland Mountain. At 7.3 miles, you'll encounter a junction with the Rough Creek Trail that leads right 2.8 miles down the southwest side of the ridge to connect with the Little River Trail.

Continuing up Sugarland Mountain, you'll find at about 9 miles an arrow carved in a tree on the left. This marks the junction of a 0.4-mile unmaintained manway that drops down to connect with the Chimney Tops Trail; the trail emerges on a point of land just before the Chimney Tops Trail switchbacks left at about 1.8 miles along its length. This is not an easy path since you must climb through rhododendron, and it's easy to get off the trail; so this path is not recommended.

From this junction, the Sugarland Mountain Trail remains level and even descends for a time, but then climbs once more. At 11.8 miles, you'll encounter a side path that leads left to the Mt. Collins Shelter. Sugarland Mountain leads up to the peak on the crest named for Robert Collins, the guide that led Swiss geographer Arnold Guyot through the Smokies in the 1800s.

At 12.1 miles you'll reach the end of the Sugarland Mountain Trail at a junction with the Appalachian Trail that leads right 3.4 miles to Clingmans Dome. Turn to the left. In just 0.2 mile, you'll reach a junction with the AT continuing straight to Newfound Gap in 4.3 miles. Turn right, and you'll walk out onto the Clingmans Dome Road across from parking for the Fork Ridge Trail, which leads down the North Carolina side of the mountains 5.2 miles to connect with the Deep Creek Trail.

# 16 Little River Trail

5.1 miles one way
Easy
Elevation gain: 1000 ft.
Cautions: Creek crossings
Campsites: #24, #30
Connections: Cucumber Gap, Huskey Gap, Goshen Prong,
Rough Creek Trails

**Attractions**: This relatively easy walk on an old roadbed keeps company with the Little River most of the way.

**Trailhead**: At 4.9 miles from the Sugarlands Visitor Center on Little River Road, turn left into Elkmont. At 1.3 miles from the Elkmont turnoff, turn left just before the Elkmont campground and at 2.0 miles stay left. At 3.0 miles, park at the turnaround where the road is gated.

**Description**: The road you follow into Elkmont is the old route of the Little River Railroad, part of the Little River Lumber Company, a major logging enterprise during the time when the forest was cut for timber. Along the road you'll pass the site of the Wonderland Hotel on the left. Built by the Wonderland Park Company, the hotel opened in 1912 to serve people riding the logging train into the mountains. Later it was a private club, and then after the park formed, it was again a hotel. With the establishment of the park, the hotel was sold to the government, but the owners received a life-time lease. In 1952 this lease was traded in for a 20-year lease that in 1972 was extended for another 20 years. At this writing, the hotel building, long past its prime, is scheduled to be demolished at the end of the lease. When you read this, it may already be gone.

Begin your hike by passing the gate and walking up the old roadbed along the Little River. Occasional benches invite you to stop and enjoy the sunshine on the violets, spring beauty, hepatica, and anemones in spring.

You may also get a chance to watch the art of fly fishing exhibited by fishermen in the river. Fishing in the hundreds of miles of streams in the park is a popular sport. The creeks and rivers harbor rainbow trout, brown trout, and bass. Fishing for the native brook trout, found in the cool streams at higher elevations, is prohibited; some streams are closed entirely to fishing to help encourage the brook trout to rebound from low numbers. Logging in the early part of the century caused runoff that polluted the waters, driving the fish from many of its streams. The rainbow and brown trout that were introduced now dominate much of the brook trout habitat. The Smokies brook trout is probably a distinct strain, but it will take more research to have it officially classified as a subspecies.

At 1.3 miles the Cucumber Gap Trail turns off to the right. This short trail leads over to another road in Elkmont; either by car shuttle or walking the roads, you can create a pleasant 5-mile loop using this first section of the Little River Trail and the Cucumber Gap Trail.

Continue straight on the Little River Trail, cross the river on an old road bridge, and at 1.7 miles you'll encounter the Huskey Gap Trail junction. The Huskey Gap Trail begins on the left here, ascends to cross Sugarland Mountain at Huskey Gap, and finally reaches its trailhead on the Newfound Gap Road in 4.1 miles.

Continue up the Little River Trail. The last time we hiked the upper reaches of this trail in early spring, we noticed a few plucked ramps along the trail and soon saw people up in the moist hollows gathering the plant; they must have dropped a few while they were moving from one picking spot to another. The ramp, a member of the lily family and also known as the wild leek, is the only plant that can be legally picked and taken from the park, but only for your personal use. You can also gather berries, nuts, and mushrooms, but again only small quantities for personal use. An annual spring festival held in Cosby celebrates the ramp, which is considered a delicacy with the taste of sweet spring onions.

Staying straight on the trail, you'll have the Little River on your right. At 2.7 miles you'll encounter another trail junction. To the right is the Goshen Prong Trail that follows along the Fish Camp Prong of the Little River and then turns up the Goshen Prong to join the Appalachian Trail on the crest of the Smokies in 7.7 miles. Where the trail turns toward the crest, the Campsite #25 Spur continues straight 0.9 mile to Campsite #25. If you hike the Goshen Prong Trail, you must ford the Little River near the beginning; it can be a dangerous crossing if the water is up.

Stay left at this junction to continue on the Little River Trail. The roadbed narrows to a slim jeep road. The river on the right dances over moss-covered stones through mature hemlocks and tangled rhododendron.

A wooden bridge takes you across Rough Creek, then old railroad ties signal a boulder crossing where a bridge crossed a smaller tributary of the Little River at one time. Campsite #24 is just ahead on the right. On a day we hiked the trail, the only inhabitant at the campsite was a deer that let us approach fairly closely.

Continue straight on the narrowing trail to a junction at 3.4 miles. Here the Rough Creek Trail turns left to join the Sugarland Mountain Trail in 2.8 miles.

Stay straight here and at 4.6 miles you'll have a creek crossing that will challenge you to keep your feet dry in the high water season. At 5.1 miles the trail ends at Three Forks, where Grouse Creek and Spud Town Branch join the Little River. Campsite #30 is nestled in the forks.

# 17 Cucumber Gap Trail

2.3 miles one way
Easy
Elevation change: 500 ft.
Cautions: Small creek crossings
Campsites: None
Connections: Little River, Jakes Creek Trails

**Attractions**: This easy trail has many spring wildflowers.

**Trailhead**: Follow the directions in Trail #16 past the Elkmont Campground to the fork at 2.0 miles from the Elkmont turnoff on Little River Road. Turn right at the fork on a one-way road through a community of cabins until in 0.4 mile you'll reach a parking area on the right. From here, walk up the road to the Jakes Creek Road on the left that has a gate across it.

**Description**: The cabins you'll pass on the way to the trailhead were built in the 1920s. At the time, memberships were sold in conjunction with the Wonderland Hotel, which had become a private club. A membership included a lot on which a cabin could be built. About 80 members took advantage of this opportunity and built summer homes. When the park was established, the homes and lots were purchased and the owners received a life lease. They were also involved in the lease trades and extensions of the Wonderland Hotel that extended their time to 1992. These cabins are also subject to demolition when the leases expire.

Proceed up the Jakes Creek Road. This is also the Jakes Creek Trail that ascends 3.3 miles to Jakes Gap. At 0.3 mile along this gravel road, you'll reach the junction with the Cucumber Gap Trail on the left. The Jakes Creek Trail continues straight ahead

After making the turn onto the Cucumber Gap Trail, you'll ascend through a stand of large tulip poplars and cross Tulip Branch on stepping stones. At 1.0 mile with a gentle ascent, you'll reach Cucumber Gap, a passageway between Burnt Mountain to the north and, to the south, Bent Arm, an appendage of Miry Ridge. In spring this saddle is covered with trout lily, spring beauty, hepatica, and many other wildflowers.

As you descend from Cucumber Gap, you'll soon walk through a passageway banked with rhododendron and fern. As the trail continues to gradually descend, you'll see a small stream meandering on your left. At 1.9 miles, the trail crosses Huskey Branch and at 2.3 miles ends at the Little River Trail. You can retrace your steps from here, or walk 1.3 miles to the left to the Little River Trailhead. You could then walk the road to get back to the trailhead for the Cucumber Gap Trail for a loop total of 5 miles.

# 18 Meigs Mountain Trail

6.0 miles one way
Easy
Elevation gain: 500 ft.
Cautions: Creek crossings
Campsites: #20, #19
Connections: Jakes Creek, Cucumber Gap, Curry Mountain,
Meigs Creek, Lumber Ridge Trails

**Attractions**: This relatively easy trail joins the Elkmont area with trails leading to The Sinks on Little River Road and the Tremont area.

**Trailhead**: Follow the directions in Trail #17 to the Jakes Creek Road.

**Description**: Walk up the Jakes Creek Road behind the gate. In 0.3 mile you'll pass the Cucumber Gap Trail on the left. Then at 0.4 mile, the Jakes Creek Trail continues straight while the Meigs Mountain Trail turns right. Meigs Mountain was named for Return Jonathan Meigs, who surveyed the line between white and Indian lands through the Smokies and who was named U.S. agent to the Cherokees in 1801. Although Meigs eventually aided in separating the Cherokees from their land, he also defended their rights at treaty conferences and encouraged them to establish their own nation.

As you turn right on the Meigs Mountain Trail, which is also a horse trail, you'll descend gently along an old road grade through mixed hardwood to cross Jakes Creek on a bridge at 0.3 mile from the beginning of the trail. The trail then ascends left from the creek to a side trail on the right that leads to a clearing that was the homesite of Lem Ownby. "Uncle Lem," as he was called, was the last life-time lease holder in the park, living at this place until he died at the age of one hundred in 1989. His old cabin was torn down.

From this side trail, continue on the main trail, which wanders along the flank of Meigs Mountain, crossing numerous small streams, about fifteen in its total length. These you can easily step across or rockhop. In spring, you'll walk through a bright forest of new green leaves, moss, and fern. This first half of the Meigs Mountain Trail wanders through a lowland that at one time was occupied by about 20 families; so along the way you'll see stone fences, wash tubs, pieces of metal, and other remnants of the former farming community.

At about 1.6 miles, you'll pass campsite #20. At 4.1 miles, the trail reaches a junction with the Curry Mountain Trail that descends 3.3 miles through Curry Gap to the Little River Road across from the Metcalf Bottoms picnic area. Beyond this junction with the Curry Mountain Trail, you'll find a side trail at 4.2 miles on the right that leads to an old community cemetery on a grassy knoll.

The trail then descends gently to campsite #19 at 4.6 miles in the vicinity of Henderson Prong. You'll then ascend to Upper Buckhorn Gap below the Meigs Mountain ridge at about 5.8 miles. With the leaves off the trees, you can glimpse Cove Mountain with its lookout tower to the northeast.

The trail then drops down to Buckhorn Gap to end at 6.0 miles at an intersection of trails. To the right, the Meigs Creek Trail drops 3.5 miles to The Sinks on the Little River. Straight ahead, the Lumber Ridge Trail passes over Lumber Ridge to the Tremont area in 4.0 miles. You'll need a car shuttle at the end of either to get back to the trailhead, or you must walk back the way you have come.

# 1⑨ Meigs Creek Trail

3.5 miles one way
Moderate
Elevation gain: 800 ft.
Cautions: Numerous creek crossings
Campsites: None
Connections: Meigs Mountain, Lumber Ridge Trails

**Attractions**: After passing numerous scenes of small waterfalls and cascades on Meigs Creek, you'll connect with trails leading to the Tremont and Elkmont areas.

**Trailhead**: Drive 11.5 miles west from the Sugarlands Visitor Center on Little River Road to the parking area on the left for The Sinks. You'll pass the parking area for the Laurel Falls/Sugarland Mountain Trailhead, the turnoff on the left to Elkmont, and the Metcalf Bottoms Picnic Area along the way.

**Description**: The Sinks is a popular attraction, a place where the Little River spills over a bedrock ledge into a rock bowl and then makes a sharp right turn to pass easily downstream. The drop in the river probably got its name from the swirling of the water, as if a sink drain has been unstopped. A portion of The Sinks was once dynamited to make it easier to get logs down the river, but it probably did little good. People enjoy sitting and watching the thrashing water and sometimes diving from a ledge into the river. You should take care, for people have drowned here in the swift current.

Once you find a parking place, walk to the right, following the trail that climbs above The Sinks. You'll then pass over a ridge and drop to an old riverbed where once the Little River meandered. Long ago, the river cut through this meander, and where it rejoined the original streambed, The Sinks was formed. You'll cross this old riverbed on stones and then follow along the abandoned meander for a short distance before crossing a small

**The Sinks**

stream. Watch for crested dwarf iris in spring and maidenhair fern.

The trail climbs a couple of hundred feet to cross a ridge. You'll then descend along a south-facing slope; with the slope's greater sun exposure, the forest is a relatively dry woods of pine and laurel.

At about one mile you'll reach Meigs Creek, which descends to join the Little River not far below The Sinks. Here is the first of many crossings of Meigs Creek and its tributaries, over fifteen. We last hiked this trail during a wet season and found some of the crossings to be quite difficult to rockhop. There are no footbridges. You might just want to wear some older shoes and wade across, but this probably should not be tried if the water is very high.

Your reward for having to crisscross Meigs Creek will be getting to see the numerous small waterfalls and cascades as the creek drops down Meigs Mountain in lush forest. The creek is tucked within banks of rhododendron. After four crossings, you'll find a ten-foot cascade where the water shoots over a smooth rock face. If you are out for just a day hike, you may want to have lunch and turn around at this attraction.

With continued creek crossings, the trail ascends, but not steeply. At about 2.0 miles, watch for a large beech tree. You'll continue to ascend through large hemlocks, rhododendron, fern, and occasional patches of crested dwarf iris with many creek crossings. Along the last part of the trail, Meigs Creek remains on your right, while you continue to cross tributaries coming in from the left.

At 3.5 miles, you'll reach the end of the trail at a junction. The Meigs Mountain Trail leads left 6.4 miles to Elkmont; the Lumber Ridge Trail leads right 4.0 miles to Tremont.

# 20 Jakes Creek/Blanket Mountain Trails

4.1 miles one way
Moderate
Elevation gain: 2250
Cautions: Creek crossings
Campsites: #27
Connections: Cucumber Gap, Meigs Mountain, Miry Ridge,
Panther Creek Trails

**Attractions**: The Jakes Creek Trail climbs to Jakes Gap where you take the Blanket Mountain Trail to the summit of Blanket Mountain.

**Trailhead**: Follow the directions in Trail #17 to the Jakes Creek Road.

**Description**: As you walk up the Jakes Creek Road, which is the beginning of the Jakes Creek Trail, you'll pass on the left the Cucumber Gap Trail in 0.3 mile and then at 0.4 mile the Meigs Mountain Trail on the right. From this last junction, continue walking up the Jakes Creek Road, which follows the old railbed out of Elkmont. The trail also serves as a horse trail.

As you continue up the trail you'll make a gradual ascent of the mountain ridge while paralleling Jakes Creek on the right. You'll cross Waterdog Branch, Newt Prong, and then Jakes Creek itself until at about 2.5 miles you'll reach campsite #27 on Jakes Creek.

The ascent from the campsite is more steep as it climbs through rhododendron and mixed hardwoods. Toward the top, watch for fringed phacelia, trout lily, and squirrel corn in spring. At 3.3 miles, the trail ends at Jakes Gap between Blanket Mountain to the north and Dripping Spring Mountain to the southeast.

You'll find a junction of trails in Jakes Gap. The Miry Ridge Trail turns left and climbs all the way to the Appalachian Trail on the crest of the Smokies near Cold Spring Knob in 4.9 miles. Straight ahead, the Panther Creek Trail drops down the mountain to connect with the Middle Prong Trail that leads into the Tremont area.

Take the Blanket Mountain Trail to the right to climb a steep 0.8 mile to the summit of Blanket Mountain. Along the way, you'll walk through mountain laurel and pass through a rhododendron tunnel. Watch for galax and trailing arbutus at the sides of the trail. Near the top you'll reach a rock outcropping offering views of the surrounding mountains.

The summit of Blanket Mountain is a grassy knoll. You'll find there the foundation of a lookout tower that once crowned the summit and beside it the remains of the watchman's cabin. Blanket Mountain received its name when Return Jonathan Meigs, Cherokee agent in the early 1800s, placed a bright blanket atop the mountain so the summit could be easily seen while he surveyed the boundary of Cherokee lands established by the Treaty of Tellico of 1798.

From the summit of Blanket Mountain, descend back to Jakes Gap. If you have a car waiting for you at Tremont, you can continue west on the Panther Creek Trail. Otherwise, return the way you came along the Jakes Creek Trail. On an afternoon when we were returning, the sky grew cloudy and rain soon fell. But then we noticed the rain drops started bouncing on the trail ahead; it was sleeting. Just out for a dayhike, we had brought raincoats but not rain pants, and below our hiking shorts our bare legs stung as the sleet turned to hail. Always be prepared for a change of weather in the Smokies.

# 21 Middle Prong/Panther Creek Trails

4.5 miles one way
Moderate
Elevation change: 2700 ft.
Cautions: Creek crossings
Campsites: None
Connections: Miry Ridge, Blanket Mountain, Jakes Creek,
Greenbrier Ridge Trails

**Attractions**: The combination of these two trails takes you to Jakes Gap and serves to connect the Tremont and Elkmont areas.

**Trailhead**: At 18.8 miles west from the Sugarlands Visitor Center on the Little River Road, you'll reach the Townsend "Y," or Wye. You can turn right to get to the community of Townsend, and of course, you can also enter the park from this direction. But continue west from the Wye on what is now Laurel Creek Road. In 0.2 mile, turn left into the Tremont area. At 2.2 miles, a side road on the right leads up to the trailhead for the West Prong Trail that leads west 2.7 miles to the Bote Mountain Trail. Just beyond this side road, a left turn leads into the Great Smoky Mountains Institute at Tremont; operated by the Great Smoky Mountains Natural History Association, this educational facility with dormitories and dining hall offers workshops to school groups and individuals on the natural and cultural resources of the Smokies. Turning here you can also pick up the Lumber Ridge Trail that leads northeast to the junction of the Meigs Mountain and Meigs Creek Trails. Past this side road, continue straight. Watch for a pullout on the right where you can pick up an auto tour guide for the Tremont area. The road becomes gravel at 2.3 miles, and you'll reach the trailhead at 5.4 miles.

**Description**: Tremont was another of the logging communities in the early part of the century. As the logging was finished in the

Elkmont area around 1926, operations were shifted to Tremont and a railroad was built up the Middle Prong of the Little River. The road you entered on is the old railbed. The Little River Lumber Company built Tremont as a company town that included, in addition to shacks for housing, a post office/store, a hotel, and an all-purpose building that served as school, church, and theater. Today, practically nothing remains of this once thriving community. Other company-built towns included Townsend, which remains as a community outside the park boundaries.

The Middle Prong Trail begins on a footbridge over Lynn Camp Prong, just above where the Lynn Camp and Thunderhead Prongs join to create the Middle Prong. The trail continues up the old railbed with the Lynn Camp Prong on the left. This section of the trail is good for wildflowers in spring; you'll see crested dwarf iris, rue anemone, trillium, and squirrel corn. At 0.5 mile, watch for where the creek spills down in stairsteps.

At 2.1 miles, a path on the right leads to the rusting hulk of an old car. At this location along the trail, you'll see blue-fringed phacelia, especially gathered around the car skeleton.

At 2.3 miles, the trail reaches the junction with the Panther Creek Trail on the left. The Middle Prong Trail continues straight for another 5.5 miles, passing a junction with the Greenbrier Ridge Trail and then campsite #28, finally ending at the Miry Ridge Trail near campsite #26. Both the Miry Ridge Trail and the Greenbrier Ridge Trail lead to the crest of the Smokies where they connect with the Appalachian Trail.

Turn left at this junction on the Panther Creek Trail, which immediately crosses Lynn Camp Prong, where you'll probably get your feet wet; we did. The crossing can be difficult at high water.

From the creek crossing, the trail climbs Timber Ridge. The trail crosses Panther Creek, canopied in rhododendron, at 2.4 miles and then twice more as you continue your ascent. The trail crosses tributary creeks and then at 4.5 miles reaches Jakes Gap. To the right, the Miry Ridge Trail heads for the AT. To the left, you can walk 0.8 mile to the summit of Blanket Mountain on the Blanket Mountain Trail. Straight ahead, the Jakes Creek Trail drops 3.3 miles to the Elkmont area.

# 22 Chestnut Top/Schoolhouse Gap Trails

6.3 miles one way
Moderate
Elevation change: 1100 ft.
Cautions: None
Campsites: None
Connections: Roundtop, Scott Mountain, Turkey Pen Ridge,
Bote Mountain Trails

**Attractions**: This excellent wildflower trail heads up Chestnut Top Lead to Schoolhouse Gap.

**Trailhead**: If you are coming from Sugarlands, follow the directions in Trail #21 and turn right at the Townsend Wye; you'll find parking for the trailhead immediately on the left. If you are entering the park from Townsend, parking for the trailhead is on the right 0.6 mile past the park entrance sign and just before the Wye. If you intend to hike up the Chestnut Top Trail and then down the Schoolhouse Gap Trail to Laurel Creek Road, you'll want to leave a car at that end, where you'll find a parking area on the right 3.7 miles west on Laurel Creek Road from the Wye. On the east side of Little River at the Wye, you can also pick up the Roundtop Trail that leads 7.6 miles east to connect with the Wear Cove Road. To get to the Roundtop Trail, you must ford the river, or if the water is up, walk back out of the park and cross the river on a bridge and then make your way down the east side of the river until you connect with the trail.

**Description**: The Chestnut Top Trail begins an immediate climb from the parking area. The first half mile is an outstanding wildflower walk in spring that is worth just going up and coming back if you only have a little time. On a sunny mid-April day we counted over 40 blooming plants and shrubs, including Solomon's-seal, purple phacelia, white erect trillium, rue anemone, chickweed, violets, toothwort, foam flower, spring beauty, cinquefoil, lousewort, and crested dwarf iris.

As you continue the ascent of the ridge, watch for a large display of fire pink at 0.2 mile and large patches of bishop's cap at 0.3 mile. At 0.5 mile the trail enters rhododendron and then rounds a point with a view of the valley of Rush Branch, a tributary of Little River. You will also see Townsend in Tuckaleechee Cove through the trees.

The trail now passes through a drier pine and laurel forest. The climb is more gentle along this often moss-lined trail. At 1.2 miles you'll top the ridge, Chestnut Top Lead, and cross over to the south slope. The trail then gradually ascends to the highest point on the trail at 2.4 miles. From this point, the trail descends with occasional ups and downs to Bryant Gap at 3.1 miles at the boundary of the park; you'll find a boundary marker set in the ground.

From Bryant Gap, the trail ascends and descends slightly to a confrontation with Chestnut Top, a tall steep-sided knoll standing atop the ridge. Fortunately the trail skirts to the left of the knoll rather than climbing it and, again with some up and down, descends to Schoolhouse Gap Road at 4.3 miles. The old road, now the Schoolhouse Gap Trail, leads up from Laurel Creek Road to Schoolhouse Gap. At this junction, you must turn right 0.2 mile to descend to Schoolhouse Gap. In the gap you'll find a dirt road that leads up from Tuckaleechee Cove beside an old house. There is also a junction here with the Scott Mountain Trail, which leads 3.6 miles west to the Indian Grave Gap and Crooked Arm Ridge Trails, parts of the Rich Mountain Loop.

At the junction of the Chestnut Top Trail and the Schoolhouse Gap Road, turn left to descend to Laurel Creek Road. At 5.2 miles on the right, you'll encounter an unmaintained manway that drops into White Oak Sink. Beyond this manway is an intersection with the Turkey Pen Ridge Trail that leads 3.4 miles west to an intersection of trails at Crib Gap. Continuing down the old roadbed, the trail follows along Spence Branch, and you'll reach Laurel Creek Road at the Schoolhouse Gap Trailhead at 6.3 miles. To the left and across the road, you can pick up the Bote Mountain Trail, which is an old roadway that leads 7 miles up the mountain to the Smokies crest at Spence Field.

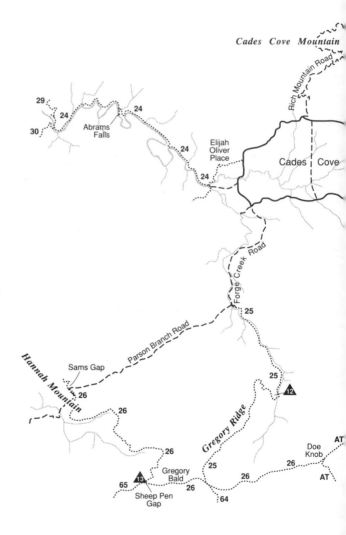

Cades Cove Mountain

29

24

30

24

Abrams
Falls

24

Elijah
Oliver
Place

24

Rich Mountain Road

Cades    Cove

24

Forge Creek Road

25

Parson Branch Road

Hannah Mountain

Sams Gap

26

26

25

12

Gregory Ridge

26

Doe
Knob

AT

25

26

26

65

13

Gregory
Bald

26

25

26

AT

Sheep Pen
Gap

64

**Cades Cove Access**

106

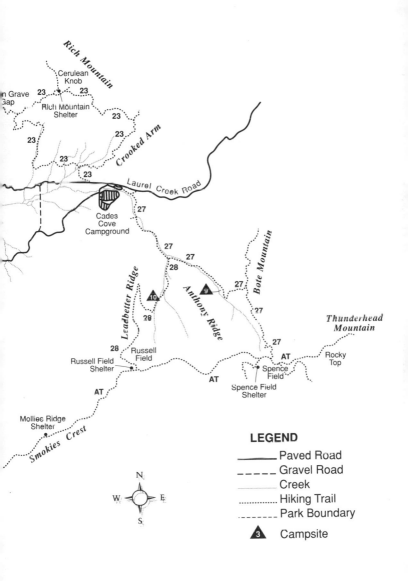

LEGEND

| | |
|---|---|
| ——— | Paved Road |
| – – – – | Gravel Road |
| ............. | Creek |
| ............... | Hiking Trail |
| – – – – – – | Park Boundary |
| ▲ 3 | Campsite |

107

# 23 Rich Mountain Loop

8.5 miles
Moderate
Elevation change: 1900 ft.
Cautions: Steep ascent, creek crossings
Campsites: Rich Mountain Shelter
Connections: Scott Mountain, Rich Mountain,
Indian Grave Gap Road Trails

**Attractions**: This trail takes you high for views into Cades Cove and descends to the John Oliver Cabin.

**Trailhead**: To get to the Cades Cove Access from the Sugarlands Visitor Center, drive 18.8 miles west on the Little River Road to the Townsend Wye and continue straight on the Laurel Creek Road. Or if you are coming from Townsend, you'll reach the Wye 0.6 mile past the park entrance sign and turn right on Laurel Creek Road. It's then 7.5 miles to the beginning of the Cades Cove Loop Road. Park at the sheltered exhibit and walk down the road for a few paces. The trailhead is on the right.

**Descriptions**: Turn right off the loop road to begin the Rich Mountain Loop. You'll ascend slightly and then parallel the road on a level trail through a pine and mixed hardwood forest. You'll find the trail broad and worn and sometimes rocky under foot.

The trail swings away from the road, passing a field on the left where you'll see a mound, which has been determined not to be of Indian origin. An old shed sits at the forest edge. You'll then cross Crooked Arm Branch and at 0.5 mile come to the beginning of the loop section of the trail. We turned right, hiking the 7.5-mile loop counterclockwise along the Crooked Arm Ridge Trail.

You'll ascend through hardwoods and white and Virginia pine, with occasional sections of the trail carpeted in needles from the pines. Crooked Arm Branch cascades below on the right side of the trail. Watch for a picturesque 30-foot cascade.

At about 0.7 mile you'll ford the creek in an easy crossing on stepping stones. This exposed, south-facing slope is relatively dry; so this trail is not especially good for wildflowers.

The trail continues to ascend Crooked Arm Ridge through several switchbacks. At 1.0 mile you'll pass through a small gap that allows a partial view of Cades Cove. A hard switchback left at about 1.2 miles provides a view down to the campground area.

You'll emerge on Crooked Arm Ridge and continue to ascend with several switchbacks. Powerlines on the right point down to the campground. The trail turns left away from the powerlines, and you'll then make a steep ascent. At a switchback right at 1.9 miles, you'll have a long view of Cades Cove, a rich farming valley completely surrounded by mountains.

In the geologic history of the Smokies, folding and faulting caused older rock to be pushed over younger rock to the northwest. Coves, such as Cades Cove, that were formed by erosion, act as "windows" through the older rock of the mountains to the younger rock below. This younger rock is primarily limestone, which makes for rich fertile valleys.

At the time white settlers entered the area, the Cherokees called the cove "Tsiyahi," or at least had a settlement there by that name. The cove came to be called "Cades Cove" after Chief Kade, a Cherokee chief about whom little is known.

White settlers arrived around the time of Calhoun's Treaty of 1819 in which the Cherokees gave up these lands. The local Cherokees who had frequented the area continued to do so after the treaty because they paid little attention to agreements in which they were not participants. But they were gradually pushed out by the whites who steadily arrived, attracted by the rich farming land. Fields were cleared; houses and barns were built. By 1850 there were 671 people living in over a hundred households. They brought cattle and hogs; raised corn, wheat, and oats along with potatoes, cabbages, carrots, onions, and eventually apples, peaches, plums; and gathered chestnuts and blackberries and blueberries in the woods.

There was postal service as early as 1833. A telephone line entered the cove in 1896. Goods were brought in from Maryville or Knoxville, first over old Indian trails, including the Indian Grave Gap Road across Rich Mountain from Tuckaleechee

Cove. The first Rich Mountain Road to Tuckaleechee was built in 1836. The Parsons Branch Road to the southwest was authorized in 1838. The Cooper Road, built around 1852, became the main link to Maryville. The present Laurel Creek Road was completed in 1922. The first car arrived in 1915, a Cadillac.

The population of the cove dropped to about 275 prior to the Civil War, and then rose to 540 in 1917. When land purchases began to be made for the national park in 1928, most people sold immediately. Many of the finest homes were destroyed before a decision was made to preserve the human history of the cove. Today, 28 structures on the National Register of Historic Places remain that represent life as it was during the period 1825-1900. Most of the wood frame houses are gone, but Cades Cove has the finest collection of pioneer homesites in the park.

At 2.1 miles along the Rich Mountain Loop, you'll encounter a junction with a short side trail to the right to a good lunch spot. At 2.6 miles, you'll reach the junction with the Scott Mountain Trail on the right. Campsite #6 is a half mile down this trail, and Schoolhouse Gap 3.1 miles farther.

From the junction, you'll climb and level off on the old Indian Grave Gap Road, which swings left below the crest of Rich Mountain. The trail is lined with galax, laurel, and serviceberry. In spring, the white serviceberry blooms were gathered to decorate the mountain churches for the spring revival service, and so the name "service." It has red berries in late summer.

The trail skirts a cove to a gap where you can see north to Tuckaleechee Cove outside the park. You'll ascend from the gap to the top of the mountain. A steep side trail to the right leads to the top of Cerulean Knob where the Rich Mountain firetower once stood. Only the foundation stones remain. Unfortunately, the surrounding trees prevent this from being a good view.

From the firetower turnoff, continue down the road, descending to the junction with the Rich Mountain Trail at 4.3 miles. The sign here says "Boundary Trail." Several trails join to make the 39-mile Boundary Trail that runs along the northwest boundary of the park west from the Sugarlands Visitor Center. These are the Cove Mountain Trail, Little Greenbrier Trail, Roundtop Trail, Chestnut Top Trail, Scott Mountain Trail, Indian Grave Gap Road, and then along the Rich Mountain Trail, which

**John Oliver Cabin**

in 2.3 miles connects with the Rich Mountain Road that begins 3 miles along the Cades Cove Loop Road as a one-way gravel road and winds over Rich Mountain into Townsend. The Boundary Trail then continues on the Ace Gap Trail for 5.6 miles to a junction with the Beard Cane Trail in the northwest corner of the park. Just down the Rich Mountain Trail from the Rich Mountain Loop, you'll find the Rich Mountain Shelter in a cove to the right.

Continuing the loop, you'll descend left from the junction. At about 5.3 miles, you'll reach an unmarked fork to the right. This is the continuation of the Indian Grave Gap Road as it heads west to join the Rich Mountain Road; along the way you'll cross Indian Grave Gap where Cherokee graves have been found.

From the fork, the loop trail descends left, leaving the road. You'll soon have a good view across Cades Cove to the Smokies crest, and then another view at 6.0 miles. You'll then descend more steeply, making several switchbacks and crossing streams on stepping stones. You'll pass hemlock and rhododendron, following Marthas Branch. The trail reaches the bottom of the mountain, and at 7.6 miles you'll arrive at the John Oliver Cabin. The cabin is easily accessible from the loop road, and so you'll probably encounter a number of sightseers.

John Oliver, along with his wife, Lucretia, and their baby daughter, Polly, are believed to be the first settlers in Cades Cove. They came in the fall of 1818 while it was still Cherokee land. They stayed at first in an Indian hut, but soon built a crude structure. They nearly starved that first winter, but the Indians brought them pumpkin to eat. Although the Indians at first helped the few white settlers, they were never accepted by the whites. Even John Oliver participated in the 1838 roundup of the Cherokees so they could be removed to the Oklahoma Territory.

The cabin that stands here today was built in 1820. A pile of stones just north of the cabin is thought to be the remains of the chimney of the first shelter.

From the John Oliver place, take the well-trod path behind the cabin that runs north. There is also a path on the west side of the cabin, but it eventually deadends. The trail behind the cabin leads back to the loop junction at 8.0 miles; you'll cross a couple of streams on stepping stones along the way. From this junction, it is then a half mile back to the parking area.

112

# 24 Abrams Falls Trail

4.2 miles one way
(Abrams Falls 2.5 miles one way)
Easy
Elevation change: 200 ft.
Cautions: Creek crossings, slippery rocks at base of falls
Campsites: None
Connections: Elijah Oliver Place, Rabbit Creek, Hannah
Mountain, Hatcher Mountain Trails

**Attractions**: One of the most popular hikes in the park, this easy trail follows Abrams Creek and passes by Abrams Falls.

**Trailhead**: To get to the Abrams Falls Trail, you must drive the 11-mile one-way auto loop through Cades Cove. Try it early in the morning; biking and jogging the loop just after sunrise, we've seen deer, wild turkey, and bear. After passing the Cooper Road Trail on the right at 4.3 miles and the path up to the Elijah Oliver Place at 4.5 miles, you'll reach the gravel road on the right that leads to the Abrams Falls Trailhead. From the end of this road in half a mile, the Abrams Falls Trail begins on the right.

**Description**: From the parking area the trail crosses a bridge over Abrams Creek, which is the primary drainage for Cades Cove. Just downstream from the bridge, Mill Creek joins Abrams. The Rabbit Creek Trail leads left from the parking area and fords Mill Creek just above this junction.

On the far side of the bridge, a second half-mile path to the Elijah Oliver Place branches to the right. Elijah Oliver was the son of the first Olivers to come to Cades Cove, John and Lucretia Oliver. Elijah bought the house in 1865. The main house, built by John Anthony, is a hewn log structure on a stone foundation; the kitchen, built by Tom Herron, was brought here and attached to the living quarters with a walkway, or a "dog trot" between. Behind the house, you'll find far back in the hollow a springhouse with wooden plumbing to bring the water from the stream behind.

113

The buildings of the homesite are located in typical fashion with the springhouse above the other structures to ensure clean water, and the barn the farthest down the slope.

At the junction with the path to the Elijah Oliver Place, bear left to stay on the Abrams Falls Trail. You'll pass through stands of rhododendron and at 0.2 mile cross a side stream on a split-log footbridge. At 0.5 mile, the trail begins a gradual ascent through pine and hemlock. At 1.0 mile, you'll top out on Arbutus Ridge about 200 feet above the creek. At this point the creek has taken a wide meander, nearly doubling back on itself.

The trail then drops from the ridge, crossing side streams and eventually reaching creek level again at 1.7 miles. The trail then ascends a small ridge at another creek meander and drops, curving right. The trail continues to descend and crosses Wilson Creek on a footbridge. You'll come to a sign at 2.5 miles directing you left to Abrams Falls. To get to the waterfall, take the trail that turns left and crosses Wilson Creek on a footbridge. You'll see Abrams Falls ahead spilling 20 feet over a rock ledge. At times of high water, the waterfall kicks up a spray that keeps the rocks at the base of the falls wet and slippery. There is a ledge that, if you use extreme caution, you can use to walk to the waterfall itself. The pool below the falls is one of the largest in the park and is often used for swimming and wading. At times of high water, it is dangerous to enter the stream.

Abrams Creek, one of the best trout streams in the park, and Abrams Falls are named for Cherokee Chief Oskuah of the Chilhowee Village that was once on the Little Tennessee River to the southwest. "Abraham," or just "Abram," was a name adopted in later life. Cades Cove was part of the land claimed by Abram and the Cherokees under him. Some say that Cades Cove was named for Chief Abram's wife, whose name was "Kate," but it's more probable that the name comes from Chief Kade.

This first part of the Abrams Falls Trail is a favorite hike and can be quite crowded on a pleasant Sunday afternoon. The more isolated remainder of the trail continues to parallel Abrams Creek on your left, climbing a couple of ridges and crossing Kreider Branch and Oak Flats Branch along the way. At 4.2 miles the trail reaches a junction with the Hannah Mountain Trail to the left and the Hatcher Mountain Trail to the right.

**Abrams Falls**

# 25 Gregory Ridge Trail

4.9 miles one way
(Gregory Bald 5.5 miles one way)
Moderate
Elevation gain: 2700 ft.
Cautions: Steady ascent, foot bridges
Campsites: #12
Connections: Gregory Bald, Long Hungry Ridge Trails

**Attractions**: This trail is one of the most popular routes by which to get to Gregory Bald, which in spring is a patchwork quilt of blooming azalea.

**Trailhead**: Follow the directions in Trail #24 to the Abrams Falls turnoff on the Cades Cove Loop Road. Continue and at 5.4 miles along the loop road, you'll reach the right turn into the Cable Mill Area, which is the largest gathering of old structures in Cades Cove, and also the Cades Cove Visitor Center. At this junction, Forge Creek Road continues straight ahead while the Cades Cove Loop Road turns left. Drive down the graveled Forge Creek Road. Along the way, you'll cross several bridges and pass the Henry Whitehead Cabin on the left and the turnoff on the right for the Parson Branch Road. You'll reach the end of Forge Creek Road in 2.2 miles where you'll find the trailhead.

**Description**: To the right, the Gregory Ridge Trail begins by leading around the base of a ridge through lush rhododendron and mountain laurel, both adding to the spring and summer floral display for which this trail is famous.

Walking upstream along Forge Creek on your right, you'll come to where Bower Creek spills down from the right at 0.3 mile to join Forge Creek. You'll then cross Forge Creek on a footbridge. We were greeted with the uncommon site of a great blue heron gliding downstream. As the trail bends to the left and starts to climb you'll see signs of an old roadbed that served this once cleared farmland in the early 1900s.

116

With Forge Creek now on your left, ascend through a thicket of rhododendron, and at 1.0 mile you'll enter a virgin forest that stretches well over a mile, hosting among it's trees, massive oaks, Eastern hemlocks, tulip poplars, and basswoods.

This forest was once dominated by the American chestnut. Specimens of the chestnut tree, once regarded as the best hardwood in America, were found in the Smokies with trunk diameters of nine to ten feet. The chestnut blight virtually eliminated this most important tree from the Smoky Mountains by the late 1930s. Decayed, moss-covered stumps and logs along this trail testify to the chestnut tree's history in this area.

At 1.6 miles an impressive tulip poplar stands just off the trail to your left. Crowded with dwarf iris, fern, and galax, the trail steepens and at 1.7 miles takes a sharp left over the creek on a footbridge. You'll then hook back left and then swing right to climb the slope passing between two colossal poplars before crossing the creek again at 1.9 miles. At 2.0 miles you'll reach campsite #12, on your right just above the creek.

The remaining three miles of the trail is steady climbing as it ascends Gregory Ridge. At 2.4 miles the trail bends sharply around large smooth boulders offering a resting place before you continue your climb through a dryer forest of pine, laurel, and maple along with sourwood, which signals the coming of fall with its dark red foliage.

At 4.9 miles the Gregory Ridge Trail ends at Rich Gap on the crest of the Smokies. At Rich Gap each fall the region's farmers corralled the stock that had been left to graze on the mountain balds during the summer for the drive back to the lowlands.

At Rich Gap, you'll find a junction with the Gregory Bald Trail. To the left, you'll reach the Appalachian Trail in 2.0 miles along the crest of the Smokies, but in just 0.1 mile, you'll pass a junction with the Long Hungry Ridge Trail that leads 4.5 miles down the North Carolina side of the mountains to connect with the Twentymile Trail out of the Twentymile Access.

To the right from the junction of the Gregory Ridge Trail with the Gregory Bald Trail, you can walk 0.6 mile to Gregory Bald, a high mountain bald famous for flowering azalea in spring. You can then continue on the Gregory Bald Trail 4.5 miles beyond Gregory Bald to its trailhead on Parson Branch Road.

# 26 Gregory Bald Trail

7.2 miles one way
(Gregory Bald 4.5 miles one way)
Moderate
Elevation gain: 2200 ft.
Cautions: Steep in places
Campsites: #13
Connections: Hannah Mountain, Wolf Ridge, Gregory Ridge,
Long Hungry Ridge, Appalachian Trails

**Attractions**: This is the shortest route and perhaps most frequently used trail to get to Gregory Bald, the largest grassy bald in the park.

**Trailhead**: Follow the directions in Trail #25 on the Forge Creek Road to the turnoff for the Parsons Branch Road, which is closed in winter. Before taking the Parsons Branch Road, remember this is an 8-mile one-way unimproved gravel road. Once you are on this road you must continue to its end where it emerges from the park on US129 near Calderwood Dam. Along the way you'll ford numerous creeks over concrete spillways, which are usually not a problem but after a recent downpour can be daunting. Once you have made it to US129, it's then a long drive around the east end of the park, but if you want to go to the Abrams Creek Access or the Foothills Parkway or the Twentymile/Fontana Access from Cades Cove, this is the way to go. Once you have made the turn onto Parsons Branch Road, in 3.2 miles you'll reach parking for the Gregory Bald Trail on the right at Sams Gap.

**Description**: Sams Gap is the crossing of the Parsons Branch Road over Hannah Mountain. At the gap the Hannah Mountain Trail leads northwest 7.6 miles across Hannah Mountain to Scott Gap where it connects with the Rabbit Creek Trail that runs between the Abrams Creek Access and Cades Cove. The Gregory Bald Trail begins on the other side of the road and heads southeast up the other part of the ridge that forms Hannah Mountain.

118

The trail climbs moderately through a forest of mixed hardwood, hemlock, and pine. This lower section of the trail is sometimes heavy in pine and laurel. At around 1.6 miles, you'll pass through a gap and ascend into a more mature forest; you'll see a few large oaks and poplars. At 1.8 miles, the trail crosses a ravine, and just after, a huge poplar stands on the right of the trail.

At 2.9 miles you'll pass through thick rhododendron, cross a trickle of water, and at 3.2 miles reach Panther Gap where the trail turns south to make the final ascent to the Smokies crest. You'll climb more steeply, cross a couple of wide, shallow streams and reach the crest at Sheep Pen Gap at 4.0 miles.

You'll find a junction here with the Wolf Ridge Trail leading straight ahead to Parson Bald, much smaller than Gregory Bald, and down the mountain to the Twentymile Access in North Carolina. At this junction you'll also find campsite #13, which has a bear locker for storing food. Turn left to continue on the Gregory Bald Trail and ascend steeply to Gregory Bald. At 4.5 miles you'll top the hill and walk out into the open grassy area of the bald, named for Russell Gregory.

Gregory is probably the most famous man in Cades Cove history. Although he was active in the community and had a house there, Gregory loved the wilderness and built a stone cabin atop the bald that came to bear his name. Each summer he tended his own and others' cattle, and he was known for his skill in summoning the herds to the top of the bald with his blowing horn. During the Civil War, Gregory, loyal to the Union although his son Charles had joined the Confederacy, organized and led the women, children, and old men in the cove to turn back a band of Confederate raiders who had been pillaging the area during 1864. Unknown to Gregory, Charles was part of the raiding party. No one was killed in the confrontation, but the raiders were turned back. Later, some of the raiders returned in the night and murdered Russell Gregory in retaliation.

The special attraction now on this highland meadow is the mid-June display of azaleas blooming red-orange, pink, peach, and sometimes yellow and white by the hundreds. On our last visit, we were caught in a downpour that slackened somewhat by the time we reached the high bald. In spite of the rain and the swirling mist, the field of blooming azalea was something to behold. If you visit the park in June, don't miss it.

Balds, which are not bare rock but rather openings in the forest, are of two types in the national park—heath balds, such as Maddron Bald in the Cosby section of the park, and grassy balds, such as Gregory. Although both types of balds occur on mountain summits and few trees grow there, they are otherwise quite different. The grassy balds are covered by a thick grass with interspersed shrubs and small trees, while heath balds are covered with an impenetrable thicket of shrubs. During the 1800s and early 1900s, the grassy balds were used as pastures by the farmers from the valleys below who would drive their cattle to the mountaintops in late spring and return to collect them with the coming of fall. No one fully understands the origin of the balds; fire, landslides, grazing have all played a part.

The grassy balds are rapidly being invaded by trees now that grazing is no longer allowed in the national park. Gregory Bald, though, has been designated an experimental research subzone within the park, where the Park Service is using various techniques, including manual clearing, to prevent the forest from reclaiming the bald. This effort is an attempt to preserve the biological diversity and scenic values of the bald. The only other bald that is maintained is Andrews Bald on the North Carolina side of the park. Gregory Bald, the largest remaining bald in the park, is also the most diverse of the grassy balds, having more rare plant species than any other.

From the bald, the Gregory Bald Trail continues west down the slope to a junction with the Gregory Ridge Trail at 5.1 miles that leads north down to the Forge Creek Road in Cades Cove. At 5.2 miles on the Gregory Bald Trail, you'll connect with the Long Hungry Ridge Trail that drops off the crest into North Carolina, and continuing along the Smokies Crest you'll connect with the Appalachian Trail near Doe Knob at 7.2 miles.

# 27 Anthony Creek/Bote Mountain Trails

5.1 miles one way
(Spence Field 5.4 miles)
(Rocky Top 6.2 miles one way)
Difficult
Elevation gain: 3000 ft.
Cautions: Steep ascent
Campsites; #9, Spence Field Shelter
Connections: Crib Gap, Russell Field, Appalachian Trails

**Attractions**: The combination of Anthony Creek and Bote Mountain Trails takes you to Spence Field where by walking to the left on the AT you'll have panoramic views.

**Trailhead**: Follow the directions in Trail #23 to Cades Cove, but rather than drive ahead on the Cades Cove Loop Road, turn left toward the campground and then immediately left into the picnic area. At the far end of the picnic area, you'll find the trailhead.

**Description**: Begin by walking around a gate and up a gravel road. You'll be walking through a mixed forest of hemlock, hardwood, and rhododendron with Anthony Creek on your right. In 0.2 mile along the road, you'll reach a junction with the Crib Gap Trail to the left that leads 1.6 miles to Crib Gap.

Continuing up the road, you'll pass through a horse camp and at 0.5 mile cross Anthony Creek on a road bridge. On the other side, you'll see a road to the right that leads to a water supply station. From here up, the road becomes more rocky. At 0.8 mile, you'll cross the creek again, this time on a footbridge, and then again on a roadbridge at 1.0 mile. The trail then ascends more steeply, crossing the Left Prong of Anthony Creek on a footbridge at 1.4 miles, just above its junction with Anthony Creek.

At 1.5 miles, you'll reach a junction with the Russell Field Trail that leads 3.5 miles up to the Appalachian Trail at the crest of the Smokies. Turn left to stay on the Anthony Creek Trail. You'll ascend now along a footpath that follows a less obvious old road. At 2.0 miles the trail crosses Anthony Creek on a footbridge.

As you continue your ascent with Anthony Creek now on your right, notice a small waterfall at about 2.1 miles. A small tributary runs under the trail, and then at 2.3 miles you'll see a large hemlock on the left growing on a rock. The trail then curves right onto an old roadbed. You'll rock hop across a small stream and reach campsite #9 at 2.8 miles.

As you ascend above the campsite, the trail turns left away from Anthony Creek. The trail is more steep as you climb the ridge of Bote Mountain, passing through coves with small streams, to a junction with the Bote Mountain Trail at 3.4 miles.

The Bote Mountain Trail is an old road that passes along the ridge of Bote Mountain. When the road from Cades Cove to Spence Field was built in the 1850s, Cherokee workers were asked which ridge the road should follow. They pointed to the mountain and said "Bote" as in "I vote for that one," except there is no "V" sound in the Cherokee language and "Bote" was as close as they could get.

To the left, the Bote Mountain Road leads 4 miles to the Laurel Creek Road, along the way connecting with the Lead Cove and Finley Cane Trails on the east that also lead to Laurel Creek Road, and the West Prong Trail on the right that leads 2.7 miles to Tremont. Turn right on the Bote Mountain Road to make your ascent to Spence Field at the crest.

At 3.5 miles, you'll reach a road turnaround. Continue straight up the ridge along an old washed-out road, and you'll reach the crest and a junction with the AT at 5.1 miles.

To the right along the AT, you'll pass a junction with the Eagle Creek Trail in 0.1 mile, down which you'll find the Spence Field Shelter in about 0.2 mile, and continue west over a knoll to connect with the Russell Field Trail in 2.6 miles. Following this route and returning to your starting point by walking down the Russell Field Trail makes a good 12.7-mile loop backpack.

To get to the bald areas of Spence Field, turn left at the junction of the Bote Mountain Trail with the AT. You'll pass along the crest in laurel, small beeches, and high grass to top a

**Spence Field**

knoll in 0.3 mile that offers views along the crest. These views are great any time of year, but get here in mid-June and you'll see mountain laurel blooming pink-white scattered all along the ridge. Spence Field is one of the largest balds in the park.

The best views are farther along at Rocky Top, an outcropping of rock on the western edge of the summit of Thunderhead Mountain. From the first knoll, you'll drop down to a junction with the Jenkins Ridge Trail to the right that leads down the ridge 6.0 miles to a junction with the Sugar Fork and Pinnacle Creek Trails on the North Carolina side. Staying on the AT, you'll climb steeply to top another knoll, drop down to a swag, and then climb steeply to Rocky Top at 1.0 mile. From Rocky Top, you'll have panoramic views of the Smokies. To the east, you can see the AT winding up to the summit of Thunderhead, which is covered with heath, so you don't get a view from the summit itself.

# 28 Russell Field Trail

3.5 miles one way
Moderate
Elevation gain: 2400 ft.
Cautions: Muddy areas
Campsites: #10, Russell Field Shelter
Connections: Anthony Creek, Appalachian Trails

**Attractions**: This short trail serves to connect the Anthony Creek Trail with the Appalachian Trail to form a backpacking loop and takes you by Russell Field.

**Trailhead**: Follow the directions in Trail #27 to the back of the Cades Cove Picnic Area and the beginning of the Anthony Creek Trail. You must then walk 1.5 miles up this trail to get to the junction with the Russell Field Trail.

**Description**: At the junction, turn right on the Russell Field Trail. You'll cross a couple of trickles and then a wide shallow stream that is a tributary of the Left Prong of Anthony Creek. At 0.6 mile, you'll cross the Left Prong itself on a footbridge. The trail crosses another tributary on stepping stones as you begin an ascent of Leadbetter Ridge.

At 0.8 mile, you'll pass campsite #10 on the right and continue the ascent. Along this section, you'll pass through a forest of large trees—buckeyes, poplars, magnolias, and farther up, oaks, maples, and hemlocks. At 1.7 miles, you'll reach the top of Leadbetter Ridge and turn left to ascend less steeply along the ridgeline. At places, the trail is lined with galax and wintergreen.

As the trail makes its final ascent toward the Smokies crest, you'll have glimpses of Cades Cove through the trees to the right at about 2.9 miles. At 3.2 miles, you'll reach Russell Field on the left, a grassy area encircled by trees that are slowly invading and will eventually reclaim the bald. The field was probably named for Russell Gregory, as was Gregory Bald.

You'll reach the Appalachian Trail at 3.5 miles where you'll find the Russell Field Shelter. To the right on the AT, you can reach the Mollies Ridge Shelter in 2.5 miles and Gregory Bald in another 5 miles. To the left, you can hike along the AT 2.6 miles to reach Spence Field and a junction with the Bote Mountain Trail. This route using the Anthony Creek and Bote Mountain Trails to reach the AT and then along the AT to the Russell Field Trail and then back down to the Anthony Creek Trail makes a good 12.7-mile backpack. Add the side excursion to Rocky Top east of Spence Field and the trip will include fantastic views.

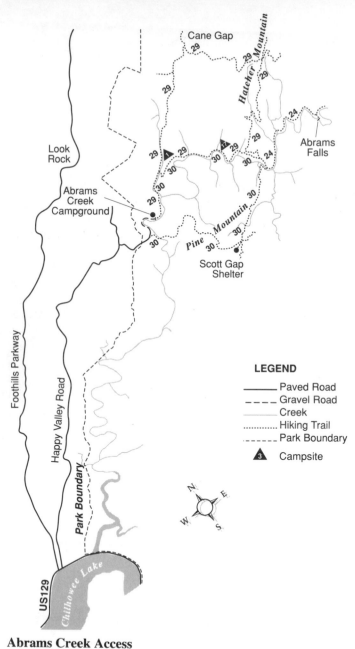

**Abrams Creek Access**

126

# 29 Cooper Road/Hatcher Mountain/Little Bottoms Loop

10.9 miles
Moderate
Elevation change: 880 ft
Cautions: Stream crossings, boggy areas, rough footing
Campsites: Abrams Creek Campground, #1, #17
Connections: Goldmine Road, Cane Creek, Beard Cane Trails

**Attractions**: This trail combination provides a loop day hike.

**Trailhead**: Take US411/129 southwest from Maryville 4 miles and turn left as US129 separates from US411; in 18 miles you'll reach the turn for the Abrams Creek Access. Or from Fontana, head northwest on NC28 to US129, or from the Parsons Branch Road out of Cades Cove on US129, continue northwest to the Abrams Creek turnoff next to the Foothills Parkway. Six miles along Happy Valley Road, you'll turn right and go one mile. The main parking area is just past the ranger station. Unless you are camping, you must park here and walk into the campground to get to the trailhead, which adds another 0.4 mile to your hike; during winter the road is closed anyway. You'll reach the trailhead at the far side of the campground.

**Description**: The trail traces the old Cooper Road through a beautiful hemlock and pine woods as it follows Abrams Creek upstream on your right. At 0.5 mile, the trail curves left away from Abrams Creek and crosses Kingfisher Creek where you'll have to rockhop. In another 20 yards it crosses the tributary again and then crosses a small stream.

At 0.9 mile you'll reach the junction with the Little Bottoms Trail to the right. This is the intersection of the loop, and so you'll finish your hike on this trail. The Cooper Road Trail continues straight, crossing small streams while gradually ascending. You'll pass campsite #1 at 1.2 miles and at 1.6 miles cross Kingfisher

127

Creek once again. You'll pass through boggy areas, and then climb to a junction at 2.6 miles with the Goldmine Road Trail that leads left 0.8 mile to the park boundary to connect with back roads outside the park. From Gold Mine Gap, the trail descends to pass through a pine woods, which is characteristic for much of this section. At 3.2 miles, you'll reach a junction with the Cane Creek Trail that leads 2.1 miles north to the park boundary. Campsite #2 is in 0.6 mile along this trail.

Stay with the Cooper Road Trail as it swings through Cane Gap and climbs steeply. At 3.4 miles you'll reach the ridgeline and at 4.9 miles an intersection, with the Cooper Road Trail continuing straight 5.6 miles to the Cades Cove Loop Road; Cooper Road was one of the main roads in and out for the cove settlers. To the left, the Beard Cane Trail leads 2.1 miles to the Ace Gap Trail that turns east to Rich Mountain.

Turn right at this intersection, now on the Hatcher Mountain Trail. You'll ascend through a pine woods and then descend along the ridge of Hatcher Mountain. At 6.5 miles you'll drop into a rhododendron cove and cross Oak Flats Branch. The trail switches back left. You'll hop another stream and at 7.2 miles cross a drier slope of pine and laurel. Then at 7.7 miles you'll reach the junction with the Little Bottoms Trail. To the left, the Hatcher Mountain Trail continues 0.2 mile to connect with the Abrams Falls and the Hannah Mountain Trails. Turn right.

The Little Bottoms Trail is a rugged, narrow trail that hugs the slope above Abrams Creek. The exposed roots and jagged rocks make the footing difficult. At 7.8 miles you'll descend to cross a small stream and then make a steep ascent. At 8.0 miles, the trail crosses a rough slide area. You'll then descend into a rhododendron cove and cross a small stream and then another before reaching creek level and campsite #17 at 8.4 miles.

The trail now passes through a bottomland, occasionally crossing small tributaries of Abrams Creek, including Mill Branch and Buck Shank Branch. At 9.5 miles, you'll ascend to top a ridge. The trail then drops down the other side until you bottom out at 9.9 miles and then cross Kingfisher Creek to the junction with the Cooper Road Trail at 10.0 miles. Turn left to walk back to the Abrams Creek Campground at 10.9 miles, and then the additional 0.4 mile to get back to the parking area.

# 3⓪ Rabbit Creek/Hannah Mountain/Little Bottoms Loop

8.1 miles
Moderate
Elevation change: 1000 ft.
Cautions: Steady climb, stream ford
Campsites: Scott Gap Shelter, #17, #1,
Abrams Creek Campground
Connections: Abrams Falls, Hatcher Mountain Trails

**Attractions**: This combination of trails also provides a loop day hike.

**Trailhead**: Follow the directions in Trail #29 to the Abrams Creek Ranger Station. Just as you get to the ranger station, the trailhead for the Rabbit Creek Trail is on the right. There's a little parking here, and you can also turn right down a dirt lane 100 yards where you can also park. But the main parking is just past the ranger station.

**Description**: From the trailhead, walk down the dirt lane to its end, and turn right. You'll hop across a small creek and parallel Abrams Creek headed downstream. You'll pass the ford for horses and a little farther find a long footbridge over Abrams Creek. Once you cross the creek, bear to your left to rejoin the main trail from the ford.

The trail gently ascends to an old homesite. You'll find the remains of a tumble-down chimney, and in spring the trail is lined with blooming daffodils. After passing through a boggy area, you'll enter a mixed hemlock, pine, and hardwood forest. At 0.3 mile, you'll begin a steeper climb that takes you above Abrams Creek on your right.

You'll follow an old roadway that once led over Pine Mountain toward Cades Cove. The trail switches left at 0.5 mile. You'll level off a couple of times, but mostly it's a steady climb

129

**Abrams Creek Ford**

130

up Pine Mountain; the woods are heavy in pine. At 1.2 miles you'll round a point and keep climbing. At 1.9 miles, the trail finally tops the ridge, curves left, and begins the descent to Scott Gap at 2.5 miles.

You'll find a five-way intersection of trails in Scott Gap. The Rabbit Creek Trail continues east 5.1 miles into Cades Cove and ends at the trailhead for the Abrams Falls Trail. To the right, the Hannah Mountain Trail leads 7.1 miles to the Parsons Branch Road to emerge across from the beginning of the Gregory Bald Trail. A sharp right at Scott Gap takes you 0.1 mile to the Scott Gap Shelter. To complete the loop walk, turn left on the Hannah Mountain Trail.

As you walk along the Hannah Mountain Trail, you'll be on a footpath, having left the old roadbed at Scott Gap. The level trail passes through a forest of moist coves with rhododendron gathered along small streams alternating with drier slopes that have pine and laurel. At 3.6 miles, the trail begins a descent toward Abrams Creek. You'll cross a small stream lined with galax at 3.8 miles. As you parallel a water course flowing down the mountain on your left, watch for a tiny waterfall at 4.0 miles where the water slides over a large boulder and drops about three feet. Also watch for huge patches of galax along this last section of trail. You'll round a point and then descend more steeply to Abrams Creek at 4.2 miles.

There is no bridge over Abrams Creek, which at this point upstream is still a wide creek. You will get your feet wet. Even in dry weather, we found it difficult to rockhop without putting our feet in the water at some point. If the water level is up, this will be a dangerous crossing and probably should not be attempted. You can always come back another day.

Once you are across the creek, you'll reach the junction with the Abrams Falls Trail at 4.3 miles. You can turn right to reach Abrams Falls in 1.7 miles. Turn left on the Hatcher Mountain Trail to complete the loop walk. You'll ascend steeply and at 4.5 miles reach a junction with the Little Bottoms Trail, which is part of the loop hike in the preceding trail description. Turn left on the Little Bottoms Trail and follow the directions in Trail #29 to complete the remaining 3.6 miles back to the Abrams Creek Ranger Station.

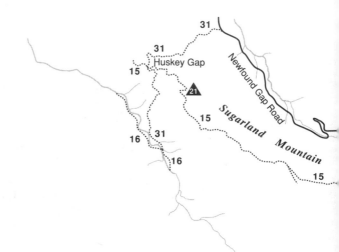

**Newfound Gap and Clingmans Dome Roads Access**

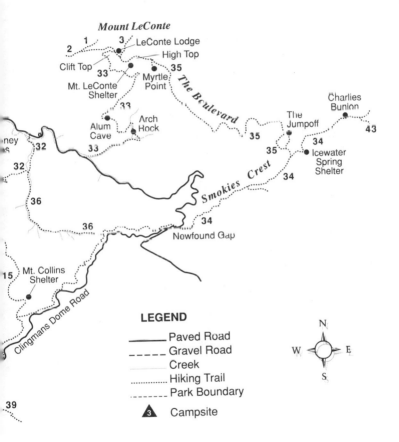

*Mount LeConte*

1
2
3 — LeConte Lodge
— High Top
Clift Top
33
Mt. LeConte
Shelter
33
Myrtle
Point
35

*The Boulevard*

Charlies
Bunion

The
Jumpoff
35
43

35
Alum
Cave
Arch
Rock
33

ney
s
32

32

36

36

*Smokies Crest*

Icewater
Spring
Shelter
34

34

34
Nowfound Gap

15 Mt. Collins
Shelter

Clingmans Dome Road

39

## LEGEND

———— Paved Road
- - - - Gravel Road
———— Creek
............ Hiking Trail
-.-.-.- Park Boundary
▲ 3  Campsite

N
W  E
S

# 31 Huskey Gap Trail

4.1 miles one way
(Husky Gap 2.0 miles one way)
Easy
Elevation change: 1300 ft.
Cautions: Road crossing at trailhead
Campsites: None
Connections: Sugarland Mountain, Little River Trails

**Attractions**: This pleasant walk to Huskey Gap in the ridge of Sugarland Mountain passes through a forest of hemlock and mixed hardwood and wildflowers in spring.

**Trailhead**: From the Sugarlands Visitor Center and Park Headquarters, continue up the Newfound Gap Road headed south into the park. The Newfound Gap Road passes 30 miles through the park, crossing the crest of the Smokies northwest to southeast and is the main route to the North Carolina side. At 1.7 miles from the Sugarlands junction of Newfound Gap Road and the Little River Road, turn into the parking area on the left. Or if you are coming from the North Carolina side of the park, you'll find the parking area on the right 11.2 miles north down the mountain from Newfound Gap. At the parking area, walk across the road to get to the Huskey Gap Trailhead on the other side of the highway.

**Description**: The trail begins with a gradual climb. As you ascend the flank of Sugarland Mountain, you'll pass through second-growth forest. This area was heavily logged by the Little River Lumber Company before the park was established, but the forest has recovered well and offers a quiet walk through the woods.

At 1.0 mile, the trail follows an old logging road to skirt a ravine through limestone boulders. Flint Rock Branch falls from the hillside on your left and passes through boulders under the trail to emerge downhill to your right.

134

At about 1.5 miles, you'll be able to look behind to your right and see English Mountain in the distance, which is outside the park. Mt. LeConte is also coming into view, looming behind you.

As the trail reaches the ridgeline, it winds around left, and at 2.0 miles, you'll reach Huskey Gap, a nondescript east-west passage across Sugarland Mountain. In the gap, the Huskey Gap Trail intersects with the Sugarland Mountain Trail. To the right on this trail, you can reach Fighting Creek Gap on Little River Road in 3.1 miles. To the left in 9.0 miles, you can climb Sugarland Mountain ridge and reach the Smokies crest at Mount Collins. When you top out, you'll intersect with the Appalachian Trail as it parallels the Clingmans Dome Road

For a day hike, you may want to turn around at Huskey Gap and return the way you came. Or you can continue straight ahead to complete the trail if you have a car waiting at the Little River Trailhead in the Elkmont area. The trail descends the other side of Sugarland Mountain, dropping about 600 feet in elevation. Along the way it crosses Big Medicine Branch and Phoebe Branch. The last part of the trail parallels the Little River upstream, eventually intersecting with the Little River Trail. It's then a 1.7-mile walk to the right to get to the Little River Trailhead at the end of the road above Elkmont.

# 32 Chimney Tops Trail

2.0 miles one way
Moderate
Elevation gain: 1300 ft.
Cautions: Steep ascent, steep dropoffs at the summit
Campsites: None
Connections: Road Prong Trail

**Attractions**: This very popular trail ascends to the twin rock peaks of the Chimney Tops for dramatic views of the surrounding mountains and valleys.

**Trailhead**: From the Sugarlands Visitor Center, head up Newfound Gap Road into the park, passing the turnout for the Husky Gap Trail on the left and then on the right the Chimneys Picnic Area. At 6.7 miles, you'll find parking along the road for the Chimney Tops Trail. Or from the North Carolina side, the trailhead is 6.2 miles down the mountain from Newfound Gap, Although there is a large parking space, you may have to hunt for a place on an especially nice day.

**Description**: At the trailhead, you'll find a low stone wall and a few stone steps that descend from the road. Immediately turn right, down into the woods. You'll then bear left and walk through a forest of rhododendron and hemlock and soon cross a footbridge over Walker Camp Prong just above where the Walker Camp and Road Prongs join to create the West Prong of the Little Pigeon River. You'll see Walker Camp Prong threading its way through a maze of boulders.

Rounding a bend you'll find another bridge that carries you over the Road Prong as it flows down the mountain, dropping over ledges and spillways, to join the Walker Camp Prong below. The trail turns back left and begins ascending. At 0.3 mile, you'll cross the Road Prong again on a footbridge. The trail then ascends to the right with the stream on your right.

**Chimney Tops**

At 0.8 mile, you'll cross the Road Prong once again on a footbridge, with the stream falling over rock shelves in veils below. Then at 0.9 mile, you'll reach the junction with the Road Prong Trail that continues straight, ascending the main crest of the Smokies to connect with the Appalachian Trail in 2.4 miles. Turn right to continue on the Chimney Tops Trail.

Along much of the trail you'll see thickets of rhododendron. We have yet to hike this particular trail during the blooming season in early summer, but it must be spectacular.

This next section of trail is a steep ascent where you'll need to stop occasionally for a breather. At times the footing is rough. A small stream cascades down moss-covered rock slopes on the left.

The trail passes through a long switchback and finally reaches the ridgeline. You'll then be able to see the Chimneys along the ridge to your right.

As you complete the Chimney Tops Trail, the path becomes entangled in tree roots and you must pick your way. At 2.0 miles you'll reach the base of the Chimneys, bare rock pinnacles that stand at the end of the trail. The rock is of Anakeesta Formation, a slate rock that weathers to steep ridges and pinnacles in the park. It is a relatively easy climb to the top of the Chimneys if you are agile and not afraid of heights. But use extreme caution, because the rock is crumbly and has steep dropoffs. If you don't feel up to the climb, be content with having lunch at the base. Because of the popularity of the place, you'll probably have plenty of company.

If you do make the climb, you'll have a 360-degree view of the surrounding mountains, including Mt. LeConte to the northeast, Mt. Mingus to the southeast, Sugarland Mountain to the west, and to the north, Sugarland Valley. You'll see Newfound Gap Road below. If you look around on top, you'll find a hole down through the rock, which is the chimney that has given the double-peak pinnacle its name. Under no circumstances should you try to climb down into the chimney. From Chimney Tops, return along the trail you came to get back to the parking area.

# ㉝ Alum Cave Trail

4.9 miles one way
(Alum Cave 2.5 miles one way)
(LeConte Lodge 5.0 miles one way)
Difficult
Elevation gain: 2500 ft.
Cautions: Steep ascent, slippery steps, narrow rock ledge
Campsites: LeConte Lodge, Mt. LeConte Shelter
Connections: Bullhead, Rainbow Falls, Trillium Gap,
Boulevard Trails

**Attractions**: This shortest but strenuous trail to the top of Mt. LeConte affords outstanding views as it climbs through vegetation zones past two interesting geologic formations.

**Trailhead**: South from the Sugarlands Visitor Center on Newfound Gap Road in 8.6 miles, or from the North Carolina side of the park, 4.3 miles down from Newfound Gap, you'll find Alum Cave parking on the road's east side. Unless you have lodge reservations, allow all day to hike to the top and back.

**Description**: There are two parking areas for the Alum Cave Trail, connected by a gravel path along Walker Camp Prong. Along this path you'll find the Alum Cave Trailhead. Cross the bridge over the creek to begin your hike. The moss-lined trail passes through a canopy of Rosebay rhododendron, decorated with large white flower clusters in early July, and winds through a forest of mature Eastern hemlock. Soon you'll cross another bridge, this time spanning Alum Cave Creek, and keep company with the creek, crossing it and its tributaries several times on footbridges as you begin your ascent of Mt. LeConte at about 0.5 mile. The moss-covered logs and debris along the creek are evidence of landslides. Most of the slide scars visible on Mt. LeConte date from a 1951 thunderstorm that dropped three inches of rain in less than an hour; soil on the steep slopes gave way, sending trees and rocks crashing downhill.

139

At 1.3 miles you'll turn up Styx Branch and hop the creek on stones, cross a footbridge, and climb rock stairs through Arch Rock, an Anakeesta rock formation carved by water erosion and the first of the geological attractions on this trail. Arch Rock is one of the few natural stone arches in the park.

From here the climb becomes more strenuous along a narrow path, and the hemlocks give way to spruce and fir. At 1.7 miles in a heath bald, a stone outcropping hosting the dainty sand myrtle provides a rest and an open view of Sugarland Mountain. The Catawba rhododendron on the bald open their pink flower clusters in June. At about 1.9 miles look left through a clearing and see if you can spot the window in the ridge beyond.

The last time we hiked this trail, a light rain made the rocks slippery; so we made good use of the cable provided as the slate path steepened along the bluff's edge. In 2.5 miles, the trail ascends to Alum Cave Bluffs.

The cave is actually a 100-foot rock overhang of the Anakeesta formation with a high sulfur content. We could actually smell the sulfur as we settled on an eroding rock under the bluffs to have our lunch. A sulfate form of sulfur is called "alum," hence the name. The alum is potassium aluminum sulfate. There was once a small and unsuccessful epsom salts manufacturing operation located here; epsom salts is a magnesium sulfate.

From Alum Cave, continue uphill along the bluffs and watch for a sign sending you left into the woods along the trail carved into the bluff's edge. The trail to the top of Mt. LeConte is steep with narrow footing. Cables and a prone ladder are spaced to help your climb through this zone of fir and mountain ash.

You'll approach the summit of Mt. LeConte by circling beneath Cliff Tops, the western perch from which overnighters at LeConte Lodge and the shelter traditionally witness the sunset. At 4.9 miles, you'll reach a junction with the trail to the lodge. To the left in 0.5 mile you can reach the junction with the Bullhead and Rainbow Falls Trails that descend the other side of the mountain to Cherokee Orchard. To the right, you'll reach LeConte Lodge in 0.1 mile. You'll see on the right above the lodge the spur trail that leads to Cliff Tops. The Trillium Gap Trail heads north below the lodge, and the Boulevard Trail is straight ahead, where you'll find the Mt. LeConte backcountry shelter.

140

**Alum Cave Bluffs**

# 𝟛𝟜 Charlies Bunion

4.1 miles one way
(Boulevard Trail to LeConte Lodge 2.7 miles one way)
Easy
Elevation gain: 1000 ft.
Cautions: High bluffs
Campsites: Icewater Spring Shelter
Connections: Sweat Heifer Creek, Boulevard,
Appalachian Trails

**Attractions**: This easy section of the Appalachian Trail leads to the rock promontory of Charlies Bunion and connects with the Boulevard Trail for the easiest ascent to Mt. LeConte.

**Trailhead**: You'll find the trailhead on the Smokies crest at Newfound Gap on the Newfound Gap Road, 12.9 miles from the Sugarlands Visitor Center on the Tennessee side and 15.5 miles from the Oconaluftee Visitor Center on the North Carolina side.

**Description**: The Appalachian Trail crosses the Newfound Gap Road at Newfound Gap. To the southwest, the AT parallels the Clingmans Dome Road to then head for Silers Bald and Thunderhead Mountain. You can also take the AT northeast from Newfound Gap to connect with the Boulevard Trail that leads to the top of Mt. LeConte or farther to get to Charlies Bunion. At the far northeast end of the parking area, you'll find the trailhead.

In the spring you'll begin your walk through a carpet of white fringed phacelia and ascend along a rocky trail with the summit of Mt. LeConte soon in sight off to your left. The ascent is gradual with a few ups and downs. At 1.7 miles the Sweat Heifer Creek Trail turns off to the right at a gap carpeted with spring beauty and trout lily to descend to Sweat Heifer Creek and connect with the Kephart Prong Trail in 3.7 miles. The name "Sweat Heifer" probably originated with the old-time practice of driving cattle to the crest of the Smokies during the summer months so they could graze on the grassy balds.

142

Continue your ascent on the AT to the highest point on this section of trail and drop down to a junction at 2.7 miles with the Boulevard Trail, which leads left to the summit of Mt. LeConte.

The AT continues straight, skirting southwest around Mt. Kephart, named for Horace Kephart who to came to the Smoky Mountains from the mid-West in 1904 seeking a wilderness experience. Until his death in an auto accident in 1931, he lived among the mountain people and in the area of Bryson City, North Carolina. He was an advocate of the establishment of the Great Smoky Mountains National Park during the formative years and assisted in the establishment of the Appalachian Trail through the park. Mt. Kephart was named in his honor. Kephart's study of the Appalachian mountain people, *Our Southern Highlanders*, has long been considered one ot the best regional studies of the mountain culture. Although Kephart was accurate in recording his experiences and relating the humor and spirit of the mountain people, later scholars say he neglected to take note of the participation in society and the development of leadership that occurred in such communities as Cades Cove.

As you skirt Mt. Kephart, you'll pass the Icewater Spring Shelter at 2.9 miles. You'll then follow a gradual descent to Charlies Bunion in 4.1 miles. When a group of hikers that included Horace Kephart and Charlie Conner, who was raised in the Smokemont area of the park, stopped to take a rest near the bare rock promontory, Conner took his shoe off to rest a sore foot. Kephart then said he would put Charlies' name on the map. Charlies Bunion provides spectacular views into the Tennessee side of the park that includes the Porters Creek Valley and Greenbrier Cove. The forest around the rock was destroyed by fire in 1925. Visitors to Paul Adams' camp atop Mt. LeConte watched the great fire for a week. Around the rocks, there are thousand-foot dropoffs, so you should use extreme caution.

From Charlies Bunion, the AT continues to the northeast. In just another 0.3 mile, you'll find the junction with the Dry Sluice Gap Trail, also called the "Richland Mountain Trail," that with the Bradley Fork Trail drops 8.2 miles to the Smokemont area on the North Carolina side of the park. If you are not taking one of the long circuitous routes off the AT or climbing to Mt. LeConte on the Boulevard, you'll need to return to Newfound Gap.

# 35 Boulevard Trail

5.3 miles one way
(Along AT to The Jumpoff 3.5 miles one way)
(Along AT to LeConte Lodge 8 miles one way)
Moderate
Elevation gain: 1600 ft. from Newfound Gap
Cautions: Slide areas, high bluffs, rough footing
Campsites: LeConte Lodge, Mt. LeConte Shelter
Connections: Appalachian, Trillium Gap, Alum Cave,
Bullhead, Rainbow Falls Trails

**Attractions**: This trail offers the gentlest ascent to the summit of Mt. LeConte and provides access to some of the most famous overlooks in the Smokies.

**Trailhead**: The Boulevard begins on the Appalachian Trail between Newfound Gap and Charlies Bunion and leads to LeConte Lodge on the summit of Mt. LeConte. If you are hiking to the lodge, you'll start at Newfound Gap; follow the directions in Trail #34.

**Description**: The Boulevard is a high mountain ridge connecting Mt. LeConte with the main crest of the Smokies. The Boulevard Trail that follows the ridge, is all above 5500 feet.

This is the easiest route to the top of Mt. LeConte because of the relatively small gain in elevation. Begin by hiking northeast on the Appalachian Trail toward Charlies Bunion. You'll reach the Boulevard Trail in 2.7 miles. Turn left and begin your ascent of the west flank of Mt. Kephart.

In 0.2 mile, you'll encounter a spur trail to the right marked by a sign to The Jumpoff. The rugged 0.6-mile side trail ends at a Mt. Kephart promontory affording spectacular views of Horse-shoe Mountain and Charlies Bunion. The name "Jumpoff" derives from the 1000-foot sheer drop from the overlook; take care.

After returning to the main trail, you'll soon begin a 500-foot descent that skirts the headwaters of the Walker Camp Prong. At

1.0 mile you'll then begin a gentle ascent to the summit of Mt. LeConte, passing through beech gaps and walking the ridgelines, all the while being led by a trail of wildflowers and shrubs—spring beauty, trillium, trout and bead lilies, laurel, rhododendron. You'll also pass through stands of Frasier fir and mountain ash.

When we last hiked The Boulevard, a number of trees were blocking the way in slide areas. This made negotiating the sometimes narrow trail with a pack difficult.

After your approach around the eastern side of Mt. LeConte, the trail ascends and switches back left to a sign at 4.8 miles signaling a 0.25 side trail left to Myrtle Point. This is the favorite spot to watch the sunrise if you have spent the night at LeConte Lodge or the Mt. LeConte shelter. But the view is a must any time of day. Here you'll stand on a platform of stone, adorned with pink sand myrtle blossoms in May, for a panoramic vista of the eastern half of the park.

Back at the main trail, continue your ascent of Mt. LeConte, and at 5.0 miles you'll reach High Top, the summit of Mt. LeConte at 6593 feet. No view is offered here, but tradition calls for pausing a moment to place a stone on the rockpile to the trail's left. It was a custom of the Cherokees to throw a stone on such a pile that had been started as an offering to an evil spirit.

Continue from High Top, and you'll descend to the Mt. LeConte backcountry shelter on the left at 5.2 miles. Then at 5.3 miles you'll arrive at LeConte Lodge. Straight ahead are connections to the Bullhead, Rainbow Falls, and Alum Cave Trails. Below to your right, you can pick up the Trillium Gap Trail. To your left, you'll find the short side trail that leads up to Cliff Tops, the place for watching the sunset. The view west into the park is rivaled only by that at Clingmans Dome, but a lot less crowded.

# 36 Road Prong Trail

2.4 miles one way
Difficult
Elevation loss: 1500 ft.
Cautions: Creek crossings, steep descent
Campsites: None
Connections: Appalachian, Chimney Tops Trails

**Attractions**: This steep trail follows the Road Prong as it falls steeply, making many waterfalls and cascades.

**Trailhead**: At Newfound Gap in the middle of the park, turn west on the Clingmans Dome Road, which is closed in winter. In 1.3 miles, you'll see parking for the trailhead on the right.

**Description**: An Indian trail once crossed the mountains near this location through Indian Gap. In 1839, the trail was widened to make a rough road over the mountain and for a time was called the "Oconaluftee Turnpike." When a transmountain road was proposed in this century, the old Indian Road was suggested as the route, but it turned out Newfound Gap to the east provided a better grade and so the Newfound Gap Road was built in 1930, with various changes made after the park was established.

The Road Prong Trail follows the Road Prong of the West Prong of the Little Pigeon River, the Road Prong obviously named for the old Indian Road. Almost all traces of the road are now gone. Begin your hike headed straight down the mountain from the parking area. Here you can also pick up the Appalachian Trail that leads left toward Clingmans Dome and right to Newfound Gap.

On the Road Prong Trail, you'll descend on a rocky path through a spruce-fir forest. You'll hear the creek gathering waters to your left. At 0.7 mile, the trail joins the creek, where you'll cross and be in and out of the creek until at 1.0 mile the trail climbs away from the creek over a rise. You'll have several ups and downs along this section of the trail, but overall you'll be
146

descending while paralleling the creek on your left.

At 1.7 miles, you'll see the creek plunge through a cascade and then down a 5-foot waterfall. From here on, the creek makes a delightful series of falls and cascades that hold your attention. After descending steeply down a rocky trail and passing over a small tributary, you'll rockhop the Road Prong at 2.0 miles.

As you continue to descend, now on the west side of the creek, you'll see more falls and cascades. The trail then passes through a wet area, ascends over a rise, descends to cross a trickle of water, and at 2.4 miles reaches a junction with the Chimney Tops Trail, which leads left 1.1 miles to the Chimneys. To the right, the trail leads 0.9 mile out to the Chimney Tops Trailhead on the Newfound Gap Road, where you should have a car waiting. Otherwise, it's back up the mountain.

# 37 Silers Bald

4.6 miles one way
Easy
Elevation loss: 1200 ft.
Cautions: Narrow rocky trail
Campsites: Double Spring Gap Shelter, Silers Bald Shelter
Connections: Forney Ridge, Appalachian, Goshen Prong,
Welch Ridge Trails

**Attractions**: You'll walk the ridge along the Appalachian Trail, with grand views in all directions, to reach a grassy bald.

**Trailhead**: From Newfound Gap, turn on the Clingmans Dome Road and travel 7.1 miles to the end at the Forney Ridge Parking Area, so-called because it lies on Forney Ridge which leads southwest from Clingmans Dome.

**Directions**: Clingmans Dome, at 6643 feet the highest peak in the national park, is a popular attraction. So you'll probably have to hunt for a parking place and then wade through the crowds of people that have come to walk the half-mile paved walkway to the top of the mountain. Clingmans Dome was named for Thomas Lanier Clingman, a promoter of the region, which he explored in the 1850s; he was later a U.S. Senator and a Civil War general.

At the far end of the parking area, just at the beginning of the paved walk to the observation tower, you'll find the trailhead for a connector to the Forney Ridge Trail. Follow this rocky path as it drops below the walk and then switchbacks through sandstone boulders. At 0.1 mile, you'll reach the Forney Ridge Trail junction. To the left you can get to Andrews Bald. Turn right, and head for the Appalachian Trail on the crest of the ridge. In spring, bluets lead the way as the trail ascends and soon gives you a distant view of Fontana Lake through the trees to your left.

At 0.4 mile the trail narrows as you pass through fir and spruce, and at 0.6 mile, you will reach the junction with the AT along the ridgecrest at Mt. Buckley, named for Samuel B. Buckley, a well-known naturalist who explored the region in the 1800s. A rock outcropping offers spectacular views on both sides of the mountain. North into Tennessee, you can see the town of Gatlinburg in the distance. To the northeast, Mt. LeConte rises above the ridge of Sugarland Mountain. South into North Carolina, Forney Ridge and Welch Ridge lead down to Fontana Lake.

To the right at this junction, you can walk the AT 0.3 mile to Clingmans Dome. To head for Silers Bald, turn left along the AT as it passes through stands of wild hydrangea whose white flower clusters bloom in mid-May. The trail at times coincides, at other times crisscrosses, the TN-NC state line. You'll descend through fir and spruce to a broad clearing on the side of the mountain at 0.9 mile that offers wide views to the southwest.

The trail continues to descend along the ridgeline, occasionally passing from spruce-fir woods through grassy clearings and back into woods. As you descend, you'll find some of the clearings sport bluets and trout lily in spring. At 2.5 miles, you'll descend to a junction with the Goshen Prong Trail to the right. This trail descends the Tennessee side of the mountains, leading 7.7 miles to the Little River Trail out of the Elkmont area.

Continue straight on the AT. In June along this section, you'll find Clinton's lily blooming with clusters of small white or yellow flowers on long stems. The trail descends again and at 3.0 miles reaches Double Spring Gap, where you'll find a shelter.

The trail ascends from the shelter. The forest changes from spruce-fir to hardwood. You'll pass over Jenkins Knob and at 3.7 miles enter a beech gap. Along this section of trail, you'll find serviceberry, a large shrub blooming white in May, sometimes called "sarvis," an Old English pronunciation of "service."

You'll cross other beech gaps and pass through The Narrows where the trail occasionally drops off the slender ridgeline to the right only to climb back farther down the trail. At 4.2 miles, you'll descend to a junction with the Welch Ridge Trail, which leads 7 miles southwest to High Rocks where a firetower once stood and you still get good views from the rocks. Along the way the trail connects with the Hazel Creek Trail that leads 14.0 miles down to the site of the old Proctor lumber town on Fontana Lake. The Welch Ridge Trail also connects with the Jonas Creek and Bear Creek Trails that lead southeast to the Forney Creek Trail. At the end of the Welch Trail, the Cold Spring Gap Trail leads 4 miles west to connect with the Hazel Creek Trail.

Bear right at the junction with the Welch Ridge Trail and ascend to Silers Bald at 4.6 miles. This once open bald is now surrounded by trees. But a path to the right takes you to a rocky spur that hangs over the valley of Silers Creek on the Tennessee side. You can also continue on the AT for another 0.1 mile, descending from the summit to a grassy area not yet overgrown that overs long views to the west and southwest.

Silers Bald is named for Jesse Siler who once grazed cattle on the bald, which is rapidly being invaded by trees now that grazing is no longer allowed in the national park. Only Gregory and Andrews Balds are being maintained. The other grassy balds, including Silers Bald, will one day be gone.

From Silers Bald, you can continue down the AT 0.3 mile to the Silers Bald Shelter and, beyond, a junction with the Miry Ridge Trail that descends north to the Jakes Creek Trail into Elkmont. This was the route taken in 1966 by over 200 hikers as a march in opposition to a proposed transmountain road through this region; the public resistance helped defeat the proposal. Miles west, the AT crosses over Thunderhead Mountain, passes through Spence Field, and at Doe Knob turns south to descend to Fontana Dam and leave the park. If you're not headed west from Silers Bald, you'll need to return to Clingmans Dome.

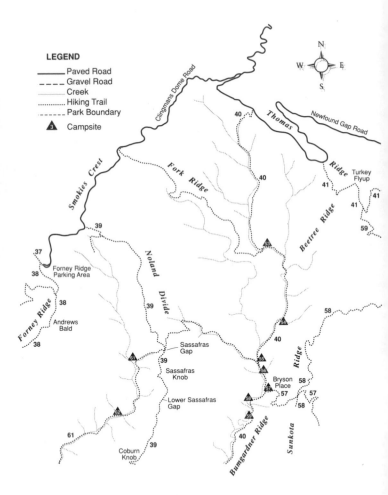

Paved Road
Gravel Road
Creek
Hiking Trail
Park Boundary

▲ 3  Campsite

Clingmans Dome Road

Newfound Gap Road

Thomas

40

40

Ridge

Turkey
Flyup

41

Beetree Ridge

41

41

59

Smokies Crest

Fork Ridge

39

37

Forney Ridge
Parking Area

38

Noland Divide

39

58

38

Forney Ridge

38

Andrews
Bald

40

38

▲ 61

39

Sassafras
Gap

▲ 55

▲ 56

58

Sassafras
Knob

Bryson
Place

57

57

▲ 57

Lower Sassafras
Gap

▲ 58

58

61

▲ 59

40

Sunkota Ridge

Coburn
Knob

39

Bumgardner Ridge

**Clingmans Dome and Newfound Gap Roads Access**

# ㍚ Forney Ridge Trail

5.6 miles one way
(Andrews Bald 2.0 miles one way)
Moderate
Elevation loss: 2600 ft.
Cautions: Rocky trail
Campsites: None
Connections: Forney Creek, Springhouse Branch Trails

**Attractions**: This walk through a grassy bald offers magnificent views and in June rhododendron and azalea in bloom.

**Trailhead**: Follow the directions in Trail #37 to the Forney Ridge Parking Area.

**Description**: At the far end of the parking area, you'll find the connector to the Forney Ridge Trail, the same trail to walk to Silers Bald. At 0.1 mile on this rocky path, you'll reach the Forney Ridge Trail junction. To the right you can reach the Appalachian Trail on the crest in 0.5 mile. Turn left toward Andrews Bald on the North Carolina side of the mountains.

You'll find this rocky trail somewhat tiring on your feet as it descends along the spine of Forney Ridge through a spruce-fir forest. At 1.0 mile you'll reach the bottom of the descent in a saddle where the trail changes from loose rock to packed dirt. At 1.1 miles, you'll reach the junction with the Forney Creek Trail on the right that descends 11 miles southwest to Fontana Lake.

To get to Andrews Bald, bear left at this junction. You'll climb through spruce-fir and at about 2.0 miles emerge into the open grassy area of the bald. At 5860 feet, Andrews is the highest bald in the park. It offers wonderful places for lying in the grass for a picnic while you gaze across the mountain ridges as far as the Nantahala National Forest south of the park. The view and the warmth on a sunny day are worth the walk any time of year. But be sure to come back in June for the displays of flame azalea and Catawba rhododendron that bloom on the bald.

**Andrews Bald**

Andrews Bald, like Gregory Bald, has been designated an experimental research subzone. These are the only balds that are managed to preserve the present plant composition and the scenic values. On all other balds, natural succession, in which the forest will eventually reclaim the open areas, is allowed to proceed.

From Andrews Bald, continue on the Forney Ridge Trail that follows the ridgeline down to Board Camp Gap and a junction with the Springhouse Branch Trail at 5.6 miles. To the left at this junction, the Springhouse Branch Trail leads 3.0 miles down to the Noland Creek Trail. To the right, this trail leads 4.0 miles west to connect with the Forney Creek Trail, which you can then take back to the Forney Ridge Trail, with many creek crossings, for a 18-mile backpack loop out of the Forney Ridge Parking Area.

# ㉟ Noland Divide Trail

11.8 miles one way
Moderate
Elevation loss: 4100 ft.
Cautions: Mudholes, overgrown in places
Campsites: Deep Creek Campground
Connections: Pole Road, Noland Creek Trails

**Attractions**: This pleasant walk along the ridge of Noland Divide takes you down the mountain to the Deep Creek Access.

**Trailhead**: On the way to the Forney Ridge Parking Area, you'll pass the trailhead for the Noland Divide Trail at 5.6 miles along the Clingmans Dome Road on the south side of the road.

**Description**: You'll begin the walk around a gate and up a jeep road that is lined with thornless blackberries in places. At 0.4 mile the road curves left past a monitoring station that is part of a national program to study the effects of acid rain. At 0.5 mile, the Noland Divide Trail turns left while the road continues on to an old water pumping station for the Clingmans Dome restrooms.

You'll now be on a footpath that at times can get overgrown in late spring and summer. This is also a horse trail but receives little horse traffic; so you don't have trampled vegetation, but you do have occasional mudholes. The hike is through a dark forest of hardwoods and spruce-fir. Because it's a dry trail, the walk is interestingly quiet, with only an occasional bird singing.

Although you'll have some ups and downs along the way, the trail generally descends along the ridge of Noland Divide. Occasionally the ridge drops away on both sides of the trail. At about 2.0 miles, the you'll descend out of the spruce-fir zone into a woods more dominated by hemlock and rhododendron. At 3.1 miles, the trail enters a rhododendron tunnel, curves left around the ridge, and enters a second tunnel. You'll encounter more rhododendron and laurel as you descend to Sassafras Gap and a junction of trails at 3.8 miles. To the left, the Pole Road Trail leads 3.3 miles down the ridge to connect with the Deep Creek Trail. To the right, the Noland Creek Trail leads 9.5 miles down the ridge to connect with Lakeview Drive out of Bryson City. The Noland Divide Trail continues straight from this junction.

The trail climbs from this gap to skirt Sassafras Knob on its west slope. You'll pass over a ridge point at 4.4 miles and descend the other side to eventually reach a smaller gap, Lower Sassafras Gap, at 5.1 miles. You'll then climb from this gap until at 5.7 miles the trail tops Coburn Knob. You'll walk along the top and then switchback left and descend through a saddle and up to the top of a knoll with an old sign that says "Lonesome Pine" at 7.6 miles. Down from this point, you'll walk along a dry, exposed ridge that provides a panoramic view south to Bryson City.

The trail then turns to follow Beaugard Ridge, which points toward Bryson City. You'll pass around and over knolls with a view to the north at 8.9 miles, finally beginning a descent toward Deep Creek. At 9.6 miles, a small cascade splashes across the trail in a hardwood forest. The trail then returns to a dry slope where in sunny spots you'll find blueberries in July. At 11.6 miles, you'll reach a bottomland along a creek where the trail curves left. You'll cross the creek on a footlog at 11.7 miles and pass a junction with the Deep Creek Horse Trail to the left. Keep straight to emerge from the woods to a parking area. Turn right to follow a gravel road out to the Deep Creek Road at 11.8 miles.

154

# ④⓪ Deep Creek Trail

13.9 miles one way
Difficult
Elevation loss: 3000 ft.
Cautions: Mudholes, stream crossings, overgrown in places
Campsites: #53, #54, #55, #56, #57, #58, #59, #60
Connections: Fork Ridge, Pole Road, Loop,
Indian Creek Trails

**Attractions**: This popular trail follows Deep Creek down the Deep Creek Valley to connect with the Deep Creek Access.

**Trailhead**: You'll reach the Deep Creek Trailhead at 1.5 miles south on the Newfound Gap Road from the Clingmans Dome turnoff or 14.0 miles north of the Oconaluftee Visitor Center. Parking is 100 yards south of the trailhead.

**Description**: From the parking area, you must walk north along Newfound Gap Road to get to the trailhead. Once on the trail, you'll descend from the road on a footpath in a lush forest of hardwoods, spruce, fir, and rhododendron. Several switchbacks and curves in the trail help in your descent toward Deep Creek, which gathers waters in the deep valley between Thomas Divide and Sunkota Ridge on the east and Fork Ridge and Noland Divide on the west. Along the trail you'll find that you regularly cross seeps and springs and small streams that sometimes run down the trail before turning to head for Deep Creek.

At 1.0 mile, you'll cross a wide shallow stream as you pass through a cove and continue your descent, now following this tributary creek downstream. You'll pass some large trees on the way. At 1.7 miles, you'll rockhop the tributary creek you have been following, near its junction with Deep Creek. From here on, the trail parallels Deep Creek on the east side all the way to its end. Although the trail has some ups and downs, it's a steady descent. Once in the bottomlands along Deep Creek, the trail often has boggy areas that you must pass through or around.

155

You'll cross a side stream on rocks at 2.2 miles. Then watch for a giant chestnut snag and a huge poplar. After several more small stream crossings, you'll reach campsite #53 at Poke Patch and a junction with the Fork Ridge Trail at 4.0 miles. The Fork Ridge Trail turns right to cross Deep Creek on a footbridge and then climb to the Clingmans Dome Road in 5.2 miles.

Walk straight through the campsite to stay on the Deep Creek Trail. You'll pass several large hemlocks and at 4.6 miles cross a side stream where moss-covered rocks jut out to the creek, a good place for lunch. Although the trail brushes Deep Creek frequently, it never crosses the creek.

At 4.8 miles, the trail crosses Cherry Creek where you must ford, or upstream you'll see a place to rockhop while holding on to rhododendron branches. At about 5.0 miles, the trail passes along Deep Creek with a rock wall on the left. Beetree Creek, which you must rockhop, flows out of the rocks at 5.1 miles. The trail then moves back to a woodland environment where it passes between two large poplars at 5.5 miles.

At 5.7 miles, a side stream runs through a metal culvert under the trail. Just beyond, you'll see that a side trail leads to the left. You should turn left here. If you continue straight, you'll find the trail deadends at the water's edge where the creek has meandered across the trail and washed it away. By taking the side trail, you'll climb above and around this area and then descend to rejoin the trail at 5.8 miles.

Then at 6.4 miles the trail crosses Nettle Creek in three branches and arrives at campsite #54. Continuing down the trail, you'll pass campsite #55 at 7.3 miles to a junction with the Pole Road Trail that crosses Deep Creek on a long footbridge to the right and leads 3.3 miles to connect with the Noland Divide Trail. From this point on down, the Deep Creek Trail is also a horse trail; so now you'll encounter long mud runs where the horses have churned the boggy areas to slush.

Just at the junction, you'll see the trail goes straight ahead with a more used path up to the left. Make the turn left; the trail straight leads to the creek's uncertain edge. To the left, you'll climb above and around this stretch and descend to regain the main route at 7.6 miles. At 7.8 miles, you'll pass campsite #56 and then cross Elliot Cove Branch on a footlog at 7.9 miles.

**Deep Creek**

Then at 8.0 miles, the trail curves left up to a level area that is campsite #57 at Bryson Place; the trail straight at this left curve is just a side trail to more camping spots. Bryson Place was once the site of a cabin of the Bryson family. It was Col. Thad Bryson who laid out the town lots for Bryson City. At the campsite, the trail connects with the Martins Gap Trail that leads left to the top of Sunkota Ridge in 1.5 miles.

From this junction, the trail crosses a side creek and then you'll see the campsite's horse corral above on the left and an old housesite on the right. If you follow the side path down by the housesite into the bottoms you'll arrive at a small memorial made of a millstone and rock and dedicated to Horace Kephart, who came to live in these mountains around 1910 and later wrote of the mountain people. Bryson Place was a favorite spot for Kephart, who had his last permanent camp here. The memorial was erected by the Kephart Troop of the Bryson City Boy Scouts.

Continuing on the Deep Creek Trail, you'll reach campsite #58 at 8.9 miles where the trail curves left. You'll then cross some small streams and climb over a rise to descend to campsite #59 at 9.4 miles. After crossing several trickles of water and many mudholes, the trail drops to a left turn where there was once a path to the right. At 10.8 miles, the trail curves to the right onto an old roadbed that ascends Bumgardner Ridge. You'll reach the ridgeline and then curve left to ascend along the ridge, crossing over at 11.1 miles and descending into a cove where for the first time the sound of Deep Creek fades. You'll bottom out at 11.9 miles, once more back at Deep Creek; here rests campsite #60.

You'll then cross Bumgardner Branch on a footlog and ascend along the slope of a ridge and descend to a junction with the Deep Creek Road at a turnaround at 12.3 miles. The gravel road at this point is closed to traffic. Turn left on the road to stay on the Deep Creek Trail, and at 12.7 miles you'll reach Jenkins Place where the Loop Trail leads to the left 1.0 mile over Sunkota Ridge to connect with the Indian Creek Trail.

Continue straight and you'll cross a road bridge over Deep Creek. You'll cross Deep Creek again on a road bridge and then cross Indian Creek on a bridge to a junction with the Indian Creek Trail to the left. Stay straight and its another 0.7 mile to the Deep Creek Trailhead just north of the Deep Creek Campground.

# 41 Kanati Fork Trail via Thomas Divide Trail

4.7 miles one way
Moderate
Elevation loss: 2200 ft.
Cautions: Creek crossings
Campsites: none
Connections: Thomas Divide, Kephart Prong Trails

**Attractions**: This pleasant walk starts along the ridge, drops through rhododendron and laurel, and follows Kanati Fork to the Newfound Gap Road.

**Trailhead**: Travel 12.1 miles north of the Oconaluftee Visitor Center on the Newfound Gap Road, or 3.4 miles south of Newfound Gap if you are coming from the Tennessee side, to the Thomas Divide Trailhead on the west side of the road. If you intend to do a car shuttle, you'll need to leave a car at the far end of the Kanati Fork Trail, which is 4.9 miles south on Newfound Gap Road from this point; park at the quiet walkway on the east side of the road.

**Description**: Climb the hill above the parking area to the Thomas Divide Trail. You'll ascend gently through hemlock and rhododendron to walk the grass- and birch-covered Thomas Ridge, named for Will Thomas, the white man who helped the Eastern Band of the Cherokees to secure lands on which to live.

Switchback left at 0.5 mile and walk along the narrow Beetree Ridge. At 1.1 miles the trail bears right at Turkey Flyup, the highest point on the Thomas Divide Trail at 5080 feet. The story is that this was a good spot for hunters to flush wild turkeys. To the north through the trees you can see Mt. Kephart.

Descend gently along the galax-lined trail, with Beetree Ridge off to your right. At 1.7 miles you'll reach the Kanati Fork Trail junction. The Thomas Divide Trail continues straight 3.2

miles to meet the Sunkota Ridge Trail, then a little farther to connect with the Newton Bald Trail, and finally to descend another 8.6 miles to the Deep Creek Access at the park's southern boundary.

Turn left at this junction to hike the Kanati Fork Trail. You'll begin a descent of the Kanati Fork Valley, switching back left through a forest of mixed hardwoods and wildflowers that include trillium, wild oats, and wild hydrangea.

At 3.8 miles you'll pass through a laurel thicket giving way to rhododendron then drop under a hemlock canopy to a creek crossing at 4.1 miles. At 4.3 miles you'll cross two small branches. Watch for showy orchis along the trail in late April and early May. Listen for Kanati Fork, which comes into sight to your right as it tumbles its way toward and eventually passes under Newfound Gap Road.

At 4.4 miles you'll cross the last branch and follow Kanati Fork to the trailhead on the road at 4.7 miles. From here it's possible to pick up the Kephart Prong Trail by walking south 0.4 mile down Newfound Gap Road to the trailhead on the left.

# 42 Kephart Prong/Grassy Branch Trails

4.5 miles one way
Moderate
Elevation gain: 2570 feet
Cautions: Narrow footbridges, creek crossings
Campsites: Kephart shelter
Connections: Kanati Fork, Sweat Heifer Creek,
Dry Sluice Gap Trails

**Attractions**: This trail climbs along Kephart Prong through an old CCC camp to connect with the Dry Sluice Gap Trail that can be used to connect with the AT or with Smokemont.

**Trailhead**: You'll find the trailhead for the Kephart Prong Trail on the Newfound Gap Road 6.8 miles north of the Oconaluftee

Visitor Center, or 8.7 miles south of Newfound Gap. Parking is on the east side of the road.

**Description**: From the trailhead parking area, you can walk 0.4 mile up the road to reach the beginning of the Kanati Fork Trail on the left. But to walk the Kephart Prong Trail, pass beyond the gate at the parking area. You'll immediately cross a bridge over the Oconaluftee River that flows down the North Carolina side of the mountains. You'll parallel the river, which is now on the left, through a hardwood forest with rhododendron.

You'll soon turn right on an old jeep road with Kephart Prong now on your left. Just beyond, Kephart Prong, Beech Flats Prong, and Kanati Fork converge to create the Oconaluftee River. At about 0.2 mile, you'll reach the site of an old Civilian Conservation Corps camp. You'll see large boxwood shrubs that mark what was once a front yard. Only foundations remain with rusting pots and utensils scattered around. You'll also find the stone frame for the camp sign, the remains of a water fountain, and a tall stone chimney. The CCC during the 1930s had 17 camps scattered throughout the Smokies; the young men in the camps had the job of constructing trails, fire roads, and visitor facilities for the new park.

At about 0.3 mile, the trail turns left to ford Kephart Prong, but continue straight to get to a footlog crossing. You'll make a sharp left to get to the bridge; straight ahead, a trail has been worn that deadends; so if you miss the turn, you'll need to backtrack. The path crosses the footlog, which has no handrail. On the other side of the creek, you'll find a deteriorating paved trail that connected the CCC camp with a fish hatchery upstream. The trail climbs a steady grade and at 0.5 mile passes through the old hatchery site. You'll see foundation remains and more domestic plants that still grow on the forest floor. Watch for the structure high on the left that may have once been a cistern.

At 0.6 mile, the trail once again fords Kephart Prong. But to keep your feet dry, continue to the left to a log bridge over the creek. Now on your left again, Kephart Prong drops through boulders and slides through pools of cold water. At about 0.8 mile you'll see old rails beside the trail; this was once an old railroad bed. Champion Fibre Company, the largest timbering operation

161

**Crossing Kephart Prong**

in the Smokies in the early part of the century, had a rail line up Kephart Prong for hauling the trees out of the mountains.

The trail fords the creek, but again you can find a footbridge to the right. You'll continue a steady gradual climb until the trail fords the creek for the last time at 1.4 miles; you'll find a footlog over the creek on the left. As you continue up the creek, you'll see where Sweat Heifer Creek comes in from the left to join Kephart Prong.

At 2.0 miles, you'll reach the end of the Kephart Prong Trail and the Kephart Shelter. This is also the junction of two trails. To the left, over the creek, the Sweat Heifer Creek Trail continues a climb up to the crest of the Smokies to join the Appalachian Trail in 3.7 miles. If you take this route, you can then turn left on the AT to reach Newfound Gap in another 1.7 miles.

To the right, take the Grassy Branch Trail 2.5 miles to get to the Dry Sluice Gap Trail. As you start up the trail, side paths lead left and right, but stay straight ahead. The trail becomes more steep as it ascends Richland Mountain. It also becomes more narrow as the railroad grade veers off to the left.

At 3.0 miles from the beginning of the Kephart Prong Trail, the Grassy Branch Trail crosses Lower Grassy Branch just above where Upper and Lower Grassy Branches converge to create Kephart Prong. From here you will enter a drier forest of overhanging laurel topped by birch, maple, and beech. At 3.4 miles the trail switchbacks right and leads up through a tunnel of rhododendron and laurel; moss and ferns line the trail.

At 4.0 miles, the trail enters a grassy area, from which the creeks and the trail get their names. You'll then cross the headwaters of Lower Grassy Branch. Watch for views on the right of the Kephart Prong Valley and then Thomas Divide beyond. You'll ascend through laurel and rhododendron and at 4.5 miles reach the ridge of Richland Mountain at a junction with the Dry Sluice Gap Trail, also called the "Richland Mountain Trail."

To the left, the trail climbs Richland Mountain to connect with the AT in 1.3 miles at Dry Sluice Gap. This is just east of Charlies Bunion. To the right, the trail drops 2.8 miles to the Bradley Fork Trail, which leads to the Smokemont Access in a total of 6.9 miles.

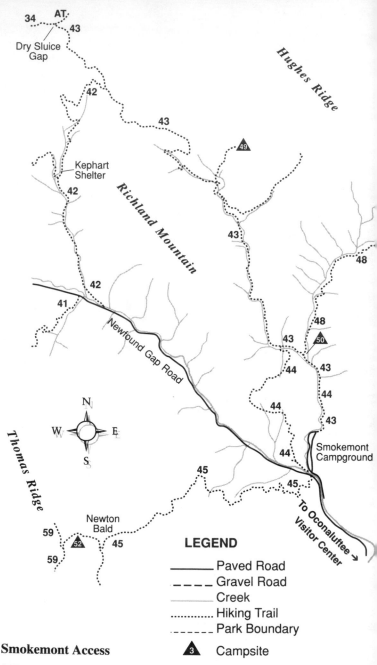

**Smokemont Access**

# 43 Bradley Fork/Dry Sluice Gap Trails

8.2 miles one way
Moderate
Elevation loss: 2900 feet
Cautions: Muddy sections, creek crossings
Campsites: Smokemont Campground, #50, #49
Connections: Chasteen Creek, Smokemont Loop, Taywa
Creek, Cabin Flats, Grassy Branch, Appalachian Trails

**Attractions**: The Bradley Fork and Dry Sluice Gap Trails connect Smokemont with the AT on the crest of the Smokies.

**Trailhead**: You can reach the Smokemont Access on Newfound Gap Road 3.1 miles north of the Oconaluftee Visitor Center or south 12.4 miles from Newfound Gap. Turn east into the campground, and after crossing the Oconaluftee River turn left and keep right to the far end of the campground at a gated road.

**Description**: The Smokemont Campground occupies the site of a sawmill village operated by the Champion Fibre Company during the years they logged this part of the Smokies. From the campground, begin your walk around the gate and up the road, paralleling the Bradley Fork on your left with rocks for sunning and pools for cooling off during the summer months. The Bradley Fork of the Oconaluftee River was named for early settlers in the region; at one time Smokemont was called "Bradleytown."

At 0.4 mile you'll pass on the right a side road to the water supply for the campground. As the Bradley Fork Trail continues up the road, you'll cross a bridge over Chasteen Creek where it joins the Bradley Fork and reach a junction with the Chasteen Creek Trail at 1.2 miles. This trail ascends to connect with the Hughes Ridge Trail in 4.1 miles. The Hughes Ridge Trail then leads north to the Appalachian Trail. To the south, it is closed. Just up the Chasteen Creek Trail, you'll find campsite #50.

**Bradley Fork**

166

Continuing straight, you'll reach a junction with the Smokemont Loop to the left at 1.7 miles that crosses Bradley Fork on a narrow footbridge and loops back to the campground in 3.9 miles. The road straight then passes by an old horse camp at 2.5 miles. At 3.0 miles two bridges take you across an island in Bradley Fork to the other side of the stream. Soon a tributary runs under the trail.

You'll cross back over Bradley Fork at 3.4 miles, just at the point where Taywa Creek joins Bradley Fork on the right. Then at 4.1 miles the gravel road you have been walking on makes a bend to the right. This bend is the end of the Bradley Fork Trail and the beginning of the Taywa Creek Trail that continues along the road 3.3 miles to the Hughes Ridge Trail. This junction is also the beginning of the Dry Sluice Gap Trail, also known as the "Richland Mountain Trail."

The Dry Sluice Gap Trail continues straight ahead and soon crosses Bradley Fork on a bridge and then crosses Tennessee Branch on a footbridge. At 4.4 miles, you'll reach a junction with the Cabin Flats Trail to the right, which deadends in one mile at campsite #49. From this junction, the Dry Sluice Gap Trail soon crosses Tennessee Branch again on a footbridge and then crosses a small tributary and passes through a muddy area. At 4.5 miles the trail crosses back over Tennessee Branch. You'll begin to see large poplars in the creek's ravine to your left.

At 4.8 miles, you'll cross Tennessee Branch again and then cross and recross a tributary. Between these last two crossings, you'll find a huge tulip poplar. At 5.1 miles, the trail curves right to cross the upper part of Tennessee Branch. The trail then bends left at 5.4 miles as it begins the ascent of Richland Mountain. Watch for some large oaks on the right and then at 5.8 miles large maples on both sides of the trail and then hemlocks.

You'll ascend to the ridgeline of Richland Mountain at 6.7 miles and then ascend more gradually to a junction at 6.9 miles with the Grassy Branch Trail, which leads left down the mountain to connect with the Sweat Heifer Creek and Kephart Prong Trails. Continue straight to ascend along the ridge of Richland Mountain to top a forested knoll at 7.7 miles and then descend to connect with the AT at Dry Sluice Gap at 8.2 miles. To the left, the AT leads past Charlies Bunion to Newfound Gap Road in 4.4 miles.

# 𝟰𝟰 Smokemont Loop

5.6 miles
Easy
Elevation change: 1000 ft.
Cautions: Narrow footbridge, stream crossings
Campsites: Smokemont Campground
Connections: Bradley Fork, Chasteen Creek Trails

**Attractions**: This pleasant woodland walk offers one of the few short loop trails in the park and in spring a gathering of wildflowers, including larges patches of trailing arbutus.

**Trailhead**: Follow the directions in Trail #43 into the Smokemont Campground. Keep right past the check-in station and take the second left through the campsites. On the other side of the campground turn left and watch for parking near a bridge over Bradley Fork.

**Description**: On the day we last hiked the Smokemont Loop, we started at this lower trailhead and walked the trail clockwise. You can also start at the upper trailhead on the Bradley Fork Trail and walk counterclockwise.

From the lower trailhead, pass around a gate and cross the bridge over Bradley Fork. You'll walk along a grassy roadbed with the Oconaluftee River on your left. At 0.2 mile the trail turns right from the old road and begins a gradual ascent of the ridge of Richland Mountain. You'll pass through second-growth hardwood with laurel, fern, and galax lining the trail. Watch for a path to the left that leads a few yards down to the old Bradley Cemetery.

The trail makes several switchbacks and passes through rhododendron and crosses a couple of small springs as you continue to climb. You'll reach a level area and then ascend at 1.4 miles through a field of down chestnut logs killed by blight years ago. It was as if we had discovered the lost chestnut burial grounds. At about 1.5 miles, watch for some large chestnut oaks.

Then at 2.1 miles you'll reach the ridgeline and wind around a point on Richland Mountain. Along this section of trail, you'll find in early spring large patches of blooming trailing arbutus, a dwarf shrub that is part of the heath family. The trail begins a gradual descent and then gets steeper at 2.5 miles. At 2.6 miles, you'll pass through a gap and descend again, now headed down the northeast side of Richland Mountain with a view of Hughes Ridge and Becks Bald to the right.

As you continue your descent, you'll eventually be able to hear Bradley Fork below. At 3.4 miles you'll pass around a hemlock knob and then cross small streams at 3.5 and 3.7 miles.

You'll reach the level of Bradley Fork at the bottom of the valley and walk upstream. The trail crosses a footlog over a side stream and then at 3.9 miles turns right to cross Bradley Fork on a long, narrow footbridge. On the other side of the creek, you'll find the junction with the Bradley Fork Trail. Follow the Bradley Fork Trail 1.7 miles to the right, back to the Smokemont Campground. Once on the campground road, you'll need to turn right and walk back to your starting point at the lower trailhead.

# 45 Newton Bald Trail

5.0 miles one way
Moderate
Elevation gain: 2880 ft.
Cautions: Muddy patches
Campsites: #52
Connections: Mingus Creek, Thomas Divide Trails

**Attractions**: You'll see a bald in the last stages of invasion.

**Trailhead**: Follow the directions in Trail #44 to the Smokemont Campground; then park across from the campground entrance on the west side of Newfound Gap Road. You must then walk north about 150 yards while watching for the trail leading into the woods marked by a sign.

**Description**: The trail to Newton Bald begins by joining an old roadbed that ascends through second-growth timber. At 0.2 mile, you'll reach a junction with a horse trail coming in from the left. At 0.3 mile, you'll reach a "Y" where the foot trail temporarily separates from the horse trail. The two rejoin at 0.5 mile.

You'll continue a moderate climb, until at 0.6 mile the trail rounds a point to look northeast across the Oconaluftee River Valley. The trail then enters a lane walled in with rhododendron and laurel. At 0.8 mile, the trail passes through a gap and continues an ascent of Newton Ridge.

At 1.5 miles, a small spring sends its water across the trail. You'll switchback at the head of the ravine and climb again. The trail passes through a more open area at 1.8 miles. Then at 2.3 miles, a stream muddies the trail, and then another. You'll soon round a point and pass through a rhododendron tunnel. The trail reaches a gap at 2.7 miles and the ridgeline at 3.8 miles.

At 4.4 miles you'll ascend and then round a bend to the right at 4.9 miles to reach the top of the knoll at Newton Bald. Don't be disappointed. Newton Bald is no more. But we found it interesting, after standing on Silers and Gregory and Andrews Balds, to see how the forest can reclaim a grassy bald. Newton Bald is overgrown with small trees, and if it were not designated on maps, we would not have guessed it was a bald at one time.

A tenth of a mile farther down this trail, you'll reach the junction with the Mingus Creek Trail to the left, which follows a ridge 2.9 miles to connect with the Deeplow Gap Trail. At that junction an unmaintained path that was once an extension of the Mingus Creek Trail turns left and drops down the ridge for 2.5 miles to come out on the Newfound Gap Road at the Mingus Mill; future plans call for reopening this trail. To the right at this junction, the Deeplow Gap Trail drops down the other side of the ridge for 2.2 miles to pass a connector to the Cooper Creek Road and then continues up for another 1.5 miles to reach Deeplow Gap on the Thomas Divide Trail.

If you were to continue straight from the junction of the Newton Bald Trail and the Mingus Creek Trail, you would reach campsite #52 in 0.3 mile and the Thomas Divide Trail in another 0.2 mile. Unless you are headed one of these ways, you'll need to turn around and retrace your path back to Newfound Gap Road.

170

**Newton Bald**

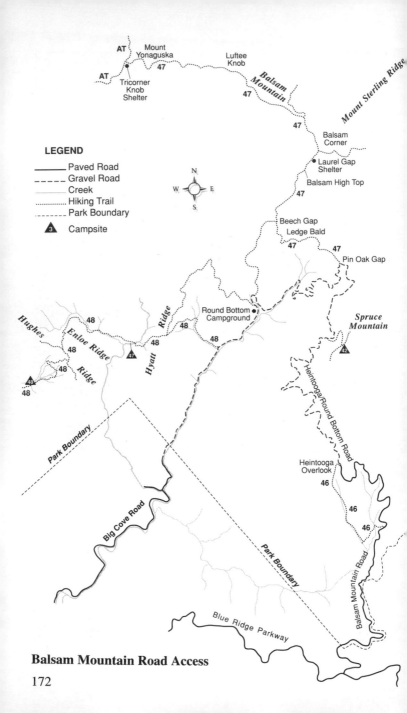

**Balsam Mountain Road Access**

172

# ㊻ Flat Creek Trail

2.6 miles one way
Easy
Elevation gain: 600 ft.
Cautions: No observation point at Flat Creek Falls
Campsites: None
Connections: None

**Attractions**: Along this hikers-only path, you'll enjoy a dayhike through a pretty woodland.

**Trailhead**: About 0.7 mile south of the Oconaluftee Visitor Center, turn east on the Blue Ridge Parkway to head toward the Balsam Mountain Access. In 11 miles, you'll reach Wolf Laurel Gap where Balsam Mountain Road turns to the north. A new name for this road is the "Heintooga Ridge Road." In 5.2 miles along this road, you'll find the trailhead for the Flat Creek Trail on the left.

**Description**: As you begin this walk, you'll drop off the road along a footpath in a hardwood-rhododendron forest. The path soon turns left and descends to a crossing of a small stream at 0.2 mile. You'll then ascend over a rise and descend to a "T" intersection at Bunches Creek at 0.4 mile. The path to the right wanders upstream and fades away. The Flat Creek Trail turns to the left at this junction.

After making the left turn, you'll cross Bunches Creek on a footlog and then ascend while following the creek downstream. The trail eventually leaves the creek and tops a ridge at 0.7 mile. Then at 0.9 mile, you'll encounter a 0.2-mile path to the left that leads to Flat Creek Falls. This side trail ends at a junction where you can turn right to get to the top of the falls; unfortunately you'll not be able to see much of the waterfall, which is a long cascade with water shooting down a narrow chute. At the junction, people have bushwhacked straight ahead in an attempt to get below the waterfall to see it, but the makeshift path is a little dangerous and should not be attempted.

Back on the Flat Creek Trail, continue straight past the side trail to Flat Creek Falls. You'll have a pleasant walk through a woodland environment of fern and grass while passing upstream along Flat Creek, a tributary of Bunches Creek.

The trail crosses a couple of trickles and then at 1.5 miles crosses Flat Creek on a footbridge and then again at 1.6 miles. Watch for wild geranium in spring. As you continue the moderate ascent, you'll enter a forest with red spruce. You'll cross a couple more wet areas, and then at 1.9 miles you'll cross Flat Creek again on a footbridge. Here, you'll see a side trail that leads to the creek, but stay straight to keep on the main trail.

Ascending, the trail reaches the ridgeline at 2.3 miles. You'll walk along the ridge and then ascend to an old road junction at 2.4 miles. To the right, the dirt road leads to an old section of the picnic area at Heintooga Overlook. Turn to the left along the road, and you'll reach the overlook, which offers views northeast into the park. Continuing along the road you will emerge on Balsam Mountain Road at 2.6 miles. Here is a turnaround at the end of the paved road and the beginning of the one-way Heintooga/Round Bottom Road, which is being renamed simply the "Balsam Mountain Road." It's 3.6 miles to your right down the Balsam Mountain Road (or Heintooga Ridge Road) to get back to the beginning of the Flat Creek Trail. On the day we made the hike, we used bicycles to make the shuttle; it's a pleasant downhill ride.

**Heintooga Overlook**

# 47 Balsam Mountain Trail

10.8 miles one way
Moderate
Elevation gain: 1500 ft.
Cautions: Mudholes, steep climbs
Campsites: Laurel Gap Shelter, Tricorner Knob Shelter
Connections: Beech Gap, Mt. Sterling Ridge, Gunter Fork,
Appalachian Trails

**Attractions**: This trail connects the Balsam Mountain Access with the Big Creek Access and the AT at the Smokies crest.

**Trailhead**: Follow the directions in Trail #46 to the Flat Creek Trail, but then continue up the Balsam Mountain Road. Along the way you'll pass the Polls Gap Trailhead where you can connect with the Hemphill Bald Trail (here considered part of the Cataloochee Divide Trail) that leads south around the southern boundary of the park, the Rough Fork Trail that leads 6.5 miles west into Cataloochee Valley, and the Polls Gap Trail that leads north 4.5 miles to Spruce Mountain. Continuing on the road, you'll pass the Balsam Mountain Campground and reach the end of the pavement at a turnaround at 8.9 miles from the beginning of the road; at this turnaround you'll find the other end of the Flat Creek Trail and the beginning of the one-way Heintooga/Round Bottom Road. Drive down this dirt road into the forest. In 5.8 miles, you'll pass on the right the 1-mile Spruce Mountain Trail that leads to the top of the ridge of Spruce Mountain to connect with the other end of the Polls Gap Trail that leads left out to the site of the old Spruce Mountain firetower. Unfortunately the path to the firetower has become overgrown; we got caught in all the briars and decided it was not worth the effort. Continuing on the road, you'll also pass the Palmer Creek Trail on the right that leads 3.3 miles east to connect with the Pretty Hollow Gap Trail into Cataloochee. At 8.2 miles from the beginning of the Heintooga/Round Bottom Road, you'll reach the Balsam Mountain Trail on the right at Pin Oak Gap.

**Description**: You'll ascend from the road on a path that follows an old roadbed up Balsam Mountain. At 0.6 mile, the trail curves right into a hemlock stand and tops a knoll to then descend. You'll pass over another knoll in hemlocks at 1.0 mile and then ascend again, this time quite steeply, to top Ledge Bald, now overgrown, at 1.9 miles.

The trail then descends a grassy slope with trillium and mayapple to a trail junction at Beech Gap at 2.3 miles. To the left, the Beech Gap Trail leads 2.5 miles back to the road near the Round Bottom area. Stay straight to continue on the Balsam Mountain Trail. From Beech Gap on up, you'll have to slog your way through mudholes if the weather has been rainy at all. Horses have helped to plow up the ground, but also the last time we hiked the trail, off-road vehicles had illegally come up from the road and had churned up the path.

From Beech Gap, the trail climbs through beech, maple, and luxurious grass to enter first spruce and then a balsam forest. At 3.5 miles, you'll pass over Balsam Hightop covered in small fir trees and descend to Laurel Gap and the Laurel Gap Shelter at 4.1 miles. The trail then ascends to a junction at 4.3 miles with the Mt. Sterling Ridge Trail that leads right along Mt. Sterling Ridge to connect with the Swallow Fork and Pretty Hollow Gap Trails and end at the Mt. Sterling firetower in 5.7 miles.

Continuing on the Balsam Mountain Trail, you'll pass along the west slope of Balsam Corner and reach a junction at 5.2 miles with the Gunter Fork Trail that leads right 4.0 miles to connect with the Camel Gap Trail that joins the Big Creek Trail out of the Big Creek Access. Continuing on the Balsam Mountain Trail, you'll follow the ridge of Balsam Mountain, passing below Luftee Knob and Mt. Yonaguska, named for the old Cherokee chief who adopted Will Thomas into the tribe; Thomas worked for the establishment of a reservation for the Eastern Band. At 10.8 miles, the Balsam Mountain Trail joins the Appalachian Trail at the crest of the Smokies at Tricorner Knob. To the left on the AT, you'll find the Tricorner Knob Shelter. To the right on the AT in 3.7 miles, you'll connect with the Snake Den Ridge Trail out of Cosby; along the way, you'll pass over Mt. Guyot, named for the Swiss geographer, Arnold Guyot, who with the support of the Smithsonian Institution mapped the Smokies around 1860.

# 48 Hyatt Ridge/Enloe Creek/ Chasteen Creek Trails

10.0 miles one way
Difficult
Elevation change: 2600 ft.
Cautions: Steep ascents and descents, rocky trail, mud holes,
stream crossings
Campsites: #47, #48, #50
Connections: Hughes Ridge, Bradley Fork Trails

**Attractions**: This long combination of trails takes you over the rushing Raven Fork and through some of the most isolated backcountry in the park to Smokemont.

**Trailhead**: Follow the directions in Trail #47 to the Balsam Mountain Trailhead and continue down the Heintooga/Round Bottom Road. You'll encounter two-way traffic and the Beech Gap Trail at 4.6 miles, the east end of the Hyatt Ridge Trail at 4.8 miles, the Round Bottom Horse Camp at 5.3 miles, and the west end of the Hyatt Ridge Trail at 6.2 miles where you'll begin this hike. You can also reach this trailhead from the Newfound Gap Road. In 1.3 miles south of the Oconaluftee Visitor Center, turn east 0.2 mile to a "T" with the Big Cove Road. Turn left again and drive 8.9 miles, passing through the northern part of the Cherokee Reservation. Just after a bridge over Raven Fork, turn right on the Straight Fork Road, which is also the east end of the Heintooga/ Round Bottom Road. In 0.9 mile the road becomes gravel and you'll then pass a gate into the park; this road is closed in winter. In 2.5 miles, you'll reach the trailhead on the left where you can park. To do a car shuttle, leave a vehicle at the Bradley Fork Trailhead in the Smokemont Campground.

**Description**: You'll begin hiking on the Hyatt Ridge Trail, first passing a gate to prevent vehicles from using this old roadbed. You'll gradually ascend Hyatt Ridge through second-growth hardwood with Hyatt Creek descending on your left. You'll cross Hyatt Creek and then a tributary on stepping stones at 0.8 mile.

At 1.1 miles, the trail makes a sharp right with a stand of hemlock on the left and soon begins a relentless uphill climb. You'll top Hyatt Ridge at 1.8 miles in Low Gap. Here the Enloe Creek Trail begins straight ahead, while the Hyatt Ridge Trail turns to the right. You can make another nice loop by continuing on the Hyatt Ridge Trail 4.7 miles as it circles back to the road near the Beech Gap Trail; you'll then have to walk back along the road to the beginning of the Hyatt Ridge Trail. The path to campsite #44 is 1.9 miles along this trail to the right.

From Low Gap, take the Enloe Creek Trail that drops down the northwest side of Hyatt Ridge. You'll walk past stands of large hemlock and hardwood and a couple of good views across to the next ridge. In time you will hear Raven Fork below. At about 2.6 miles, a small stream joins the trail, making the rocks in the trail slippery. You'll encounter unmaintained side paths to the left and then the right, but stay with the main trail until you drop past large boulders to Raven Fork at 2.8 miles. The creek is an impressive force of water that cascades through a rock-lined trough. It's a picturesque spot for a lunch break.

A bridge takes you over Raven Fork. Just on the other side you'll find campsite #47. Head left, ascending slightly and then walking level with Raven Fork on your left. At 3.0 miles, the trail begins an ascent of Enloe Ridge through large hemlocks and hardwoods. Watch for a large poplar on the left at 3.2 miles that woodpeckers have attacked with a vengeance. Beyond, you'll begin to see Enloe Creek on the left as it cascades down the hollow to join Raven Fork below. The ridge and creek are named for Abraham Enloe who came to the Oconaluftee Valley in the early 1800s. You'll pass through a section of trail that in late summer gets overgrown and in places can be muddy.

At 3.8 miles watch for a cascading waterfall and plunge pool. You'll walk along a steep bank with narrow footing. Then a small stream crosses the trail. At 3.9 miles, the trail crosses Enloe Creek. There's an extremely long and narrow footbridge here that's probably not safe to use, since it is old and high above the creek. It's better to rockhop or ford the stream. But one of us had to try the old footlog. By the time he got to the center, his

**Raven Fork Bridge**

trembling knees caused the log to shake and sway, and he wondered if he would live to write about this hike.

Once on the other side, we had to slog through a mud patch and then begin ascending from the creek, with more mudholes. This next section of trail parallels Enloe Creek on its left as it skirts the northern end of Enloe Ridge. The creek eventually drops out of sight, although you can still hear it.

At 4.5 miles the trail turns from the creek and begins a climb of Hughes Ridge, named for Ralph Hughes, another early setter in the Oconaluftee Valley. Watch for large fir and hemlock at 4.9 miles. After a couple of switchbacks, you'll then gain Hughes Ridge and a junction with the Hughes Ridge Trail at 5.4 miles.

From this junction, the Hughes Ridge Trail leads 4.7 miles right to the Appalachian Trail on the crest of the Smokies. Turn left. For the next half mile, the trail follows Hughes Ridge down through a dry ridgetop forest. At 5.9 miles, you'll reach the junction of the Chasteen Creek Trail on the right. Straight ahead, the Hughes Ridge Trail originally led 7.3 miles to the Smokemont Campground, but the trail crossed a part of the Cherokee Reservation that is now closed to hikers.

So to get to Smokemont, turn right on the Chasteen Creek Trail and begin descending the southwest side of Hughes Ridge. At 6.1 miles, you'll have a view back at the ridgeline. The descent then gets steep. In late summer you'll see asters and goldenrods.

At 6.5 miles, the trail crosses the head of a ravine and then switchbacks left to cross it again. At 7.2 miles the downhill is relentless. The trail crosses several small tributaries. The grade eases up a bit as the trail joins an old jeep road, but it's still downhill and quite rocky. At 7.8 miles, you'll reach campsite #48. Just beyond, Chasteen Creek flows under the road on its way down the mountain to join Bradley Fork.

After this, the trail levels out a bit and from then on makes a gradual descent with better footing while paralleling Chasteen Creek, which is below on the right. At 9.5 miles, watch for a double-slide falls in the creek and just beyond, a horse tie-up area. At 9.9 miles, you'll pass campsite #50 on your left. The trail then crosses a bridge back over Chasteen Creek and reaches a junction with the Bradley Fork Trail at 10.0 miles. From here it is then 1.2 miles left to the Smokemont Campground.

54
54
Pretty Hollow
Gap
Long Bunk
*Mount Sterling Ridge*
51
51
Short Bunk
52
Davidson
Gap
*Noland Mountain*
51
**39**
52
51
50
50
49
50
**40**
*Fork Ridge*
49
49
*Big*
49
**41**
49

**Cataloochee Access**

182

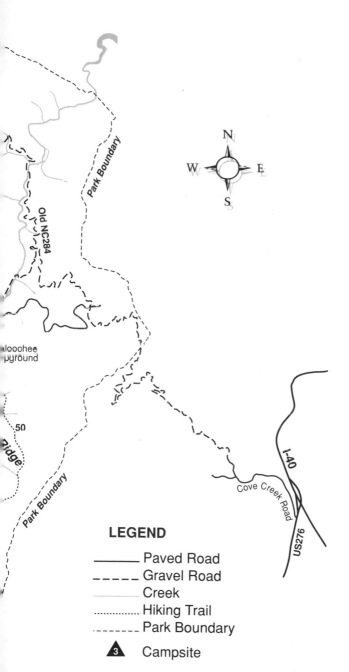

Old NC284

Park Boundary

looohee
pground

50

idge

Park Boundary

Park Boundary

Cove Creek Road

I-40

US276

**LEGEND**

——— Paved Road

----- Gravel Road

——— Creek

··········· Hiking Trail

---·---·- Park Boundary

▲ 3   Campsite

183

# 49 Rough Fork/Caldwell Fork/ Fork Ridge Loop

9.3 miles
(Woody Place 1.0 mile one way)
Moderate
Elevation Change: 1200 ft.
Cautions: Mudholes, stream crossings, steep climb
Campsites: #40, #41
Connections: Double Gap, McKee Branch Trails

**Attractions**: These three trails create a convenient loop for either backpacking or day hiking through big tree country.

**Trailhead**: On I-40, 80 miles southeast of Knoxville or 30 miles west of Asheville, take the Waynesville/Maggie Valley Exit to US276. Almost immediately turn northwest off US276 on Cove Creek Road. (If you are coming from the Oconaluftee area, take US19 east from Cherokee and then at Dellwood take US276 north to Cove Creek Road.) In 0.6 mile, you'll pass White Oak Road on the right, and at 1.3 miles bear right to stay on Cove Creek Road. At 1.5 miles the pavement ends; you'll then keep on the gravel road as it winds up the mountain. There have been proposals to pave this road, but keeping it gravel helps to ensure the peaceful isolation of the valley. At 5.8 miles you'll enter the park where the Asbury Trail leads right and the Cataloochee Divide Trail leads left. You'll encounter a paved road at 7.6 miles; you could continue straight to the Big Creek Access in 16 miles, so of course this is the way in from Big Creek and Cosby. Turn left on the paved road to drop down into Cataloochee Valley; you'll reach the campground at 10.7 miles. Continue straight; past the ranger station, the road becomes gravel once again at 12.2 miles. Keep going to the end of the road and the trailhead at 13.2 miles.

**Description**: As you drive down the road to the trailhead, you'll pass through a pastoral valley, called "Gad-a-lu-tsi" by the
184

Cherokees. Whites began entering in the early 1800s until Cataloochee contained a thriving settlement of homesteads. There were once 200 buildings scattered along the valley. By 1910, the 1200 people living in Cataloochee and the adjacent Little Cataloochee made up the largest community in the park area, twice the population of Cades Cove. Of the few buildings that remain in the two valleys, 16 are on the National Register of Historic Places. You'll pass several along the road—the Will Messer Barn just before the ranger station on the right, the Palmer Chapel on the left as the paved road becomes gravel, the Beech Grove School just after crossing Palmer Creek on a bridge, and then a barn on the right with the Caldwell House to the left. Levi Caldwell, who was probably the first to enter the valley, around 1814, lived in a log house on this location. A descendent, Hiram Caldwell, built the modern frame house in 1906.

At the end of the road, you'll walk around a gate to begin your hike up the Rough Fork Trail that parallels Rough Fork on your left. The trail follows the old roadbed while gradually ascending. At 0.5 mile the trail crosses the fork on a footbridge, and then again at 0.7 mile and 0.8 mile. At 1.0 mile, you'll reach the Woody Place, a white frame house enclosing a log cabin built sometime before the Civil War by Jonathan Woody; the house was enlarged 1901-10. Don't miss the springhouse to the right.

Continue up the trail from the Woody Place. At 1.2 miles watch for a grove of large hemlocks and poplars on the left and then two good examples of trees with prop roots—where the trees began atop a fallen tree with the roots growing around and down to the ground; once the log rotted away, the trees were left standing on their roots like stilts. The trail crosses Hurricane Creek, a tributary of Rough Fork, at 1.4 miles. You'll then find campsite #40 at 1.5 miles; the campsite is to the right on the point of land between Hurricane Creek and Rough Fork.

The trail then ascends more steeply after the campsite, still through mature woods of hemlock and poplar. You'll reach a small gap at the ridgeline of Big Fork Ridge at 2.7 miles; watch for a couple of tall chestnut snags. You'll ascend along the ridgeline to a junction with the Caldwell Fork Trail at 3.0 miles. The Rough Fork Trail continues straight for another 3.5 miles to Polls Gap and the Balsam Mountain Road. Turn left.

**Woody Place**

186

From this junction, the Caldwell Fork Trail descends through a mature forest. The trail in places has been chopped up by horse traffic. At 4.2 miles, you'll encounter a side trail that leads left to a hitching rail and the "Big Poplars," three huge poplars, the largest about 20 feet around.

Continue descending from the Big Poplars, and you'll reach campsite #41 at 4.4 miles. You'll then cross Caldwell Fork on a footbridge and ascend to a junction at 4.7 miles with the Double Gap Trail, which leads right 3.0 miles to Double Gap at a junction with the Cataloochee Divide Trail to the north and the Hemphill Bald Trail to the south. Notice to the left at your junction a pile of rocks that marks an old homesite or at least a cleared field.

Keep left at this junction with the Double Gap Trail. At 4.8 miles, you'll rockhop across Double Gap Branch. The trail crosses other small streams and gradually descends along Caldwell Fork to a junction at 6.2 miles with the McKee Branch Trail that leads right 2.3 miles to Purchase Gap on the Cataloochee Divide Trail. Continue straight another 150 yards to a junction with the Fork Ridge Trail to the left (sometimes called the "Big Fork Ridge Trail" to avoid confusion with the Fork Ridge Trail off Clingmans Dome Road). The Caldwell Fork Trail continues straight 3.3 miles to the Cataloochee Campground.

Turn left on the Fork Ridge Trail to complete the loop. You'll drop down to a crossing of Caldwell Fork on a footbridge. The trail passes through a bottomland and then curves right to begin an ascent of Rabbit Ridge in a cool hemlock woods. You'll top the ridge at 7.3 miles and then follow the ridgeline up to the top of Big Fork Ridge. At 7.6 miles the trail passes over the ridge and descends; then at 8.2 miles you'll curve right through a gap and continue the descent. The trail crosses a shallow stream, passes large hemlocks, and then descends more steeply.

At 8.9 miles, you see a spring beside the trail; the forest opens up as if this were once a field, now overgrown. Then at 9.1 miles you'll pass an old homesite on the left. At 9.3 miles the trail ends after crossing Rough Fork on a footbridge. Out at the gravel road, you must walk to the left a short distance to get back to your car. To the right Rough Fork flows along to join Palmer Creek, which meets Caldwell Fork right at the campground to form Cataloochee Creek.

# 50 Boogerman/Caldwell Fork Loop

7.4 miles
Moderate
Elevation change: 1300 ft.
Cautions: Mudholes on Caldwell Fork Trail
Campsites: Cataloochee Campground
Connections: None

**Attractions**: With the Caldwell Fork Trail, the Boogerman Trail forms a loop through some of the best stands of trees in the park.

**Trailhead**: Follow the directions in Trail #49 to the Cataloochee Campground. Just past the campground you'll find on the left the trailhead for the Caldwell Fork Trail. There's room for a vehicle to park just past the trailhead, but you might also park at the campground signup station and walk the road to the trailhead.

**Description**: At the beginning of the Caldwell Fork Trail, you'll cross Palmer Creek on a long footbridge. The trail follows an old roadbed, but then curves right through a bottomland of pine, hardwoods, and hemlocks. Bear right at a fork, and the trail soon curves left to follow Caldwell Fork. At 0.6 mile, the trail rises above the creek to a view of where Caldwell Fork makes a right-angle turn, apparently running into hard rock at the base of the rise you stand on. The trail then descends back to creek level and crosses Caldwell Fork on a footbridge at 0.7 mile. At 0.8 mile, you'll reach a left turn onto the Boogerman Trail.

The Palmers where one of the early settlers in Cataloochee, Turkey George Palmer having settled here with his family in 1848. By the time his grandson, Robert, came along a community had been established in the valley. Robert was a shy boy, and on the first day of school, when asked his name, he ducked his face into his arms on the desk and replied "the Booger Man." As a adult, seeking to get away to the seclusion of the ancient forest,

Robert Palmer built his home high on the mountainside now traversed by the Boogerman Trail.

After turning left off the Caldwell Fork Trail, you'll hop Palmer Branch and begin an ascent into large trees; most of this ridge slope was spared the lumberman's saw due to Robert Palmer's protection, and so for nearly all of the trail's distance you'll walk among big hemlocks and poplars.

The trail climbs to pass around a point that is a lower extension of Den Ridge and then at about 2.1 miles descend the other side of the ridge through a large stand of white pine. At 2.3 miles you'll cross Den Branch over an old bridge at a housesite. You'll ascend up the cove and curve right to climb to a low gap on Den Ridge at 2.5 miles and ascend along a rail fence.

The trail crosses several small streams, some nonexistent in dry weather, and then dips to cross Sag Branch at 3.0 miles. You'll see a wagon wheel lying on the right. You'll then ascend steeply over a ridge at 3.2 miles and descend, passing large chestnut oaks and black gum and down chestnut logs. You'll cross a small stream and then pass through an old gateway that has only the side posts remaining. The trail then skirts a long rock wall on the right that's three feet high and two feet thick. You'll pass large poplars, one with a cavity you can walk in.

Then at 4.0 miles, the trail crosses Snake Branch and follows an old roadbed downstream. At 4.2 miles, you'll cross back over Snake Branch and follow another roadbed down the creek. The trail passes a small waterfall and then fence posts between road and creek. At 4.4 miles, the remains of a log building are to the right, and then at 4.5 miles you'll cross Snake Branch again.

The trail then climbs from the creek over a rise to a housesite on the left with a basement. At 4.6 miles the Boogerman Trail rejoins the Caldwell Fork Trail. To the left, the Caldwell Fork Trail leads half a mile to the junction with the Fork Ridge Trail and then on up to the Rough Fork Trail. Turn right to complete the loop back to the campground. At 6.6 miles, you'll return to the beginning of the Boogerman Trail, along the way crossing Snake Branch and then Caldwell Fork and small tributaries 13 times on footbridges. You'll also have to skirt around mudholes churned up by horse traffic. Once back to the beginning of the Boogerman Trail, keep straight to return to your starting point.

**Tree Cavity**

190

# 51 Pretty Hollow Gap Trail

5.3 miles one way
Moderate
Elevation gain: 2400 ft.
Cautions: Steady climb
Campsites: #39
Connections: Little Cataloochee, Palmer Creek,
Mt. Sterling Ridge, Swallow Fork Trails

**Attractions**: This trail gives access to Little Cataloochee and connects the Cataloochee Access with the Big Creek Access.

**Trailhead**: Follow the directions in Trail #49 past the ranger station where the paved Cataloochee Road becomes gravel. A short distance beyond, you'll find the Pretty Hollow Gap Trailhead on the right just before the road crosses a bridge over Palmer Creek.

**Description**: Begin your walk by passing around the gate that blocks access up the old road that is the Pretty Hollow Gap Trail. At 0.2 mile, you'll pass a horse camp on the right; those that have reservations here gain access through the gate. Just beyond the camp, you'll pass through another gate that prevents continued access up the trail.

The old road makes a gradual ascent as it parallels Palmer Creek on the left, going upstream. At 0.5 mile watch for a log forming a small dam in the river; the pool behind makes a great swimming hole. The trail then climbs more steeply over a rise where there has been a slide, but the road is repaired. You'll descend and then resume your gradual climb. At 0.8 mile, you'll reach a junction with the Little Cataloochee Trail to the right that passes over a ridge into Little Cataloochee Valley.

Continue straight on the old road. You'll cross Davidson Branch at 0.9 mile and then at 1.3 miles reach a junction with the Palmer Creek Trail on the left near the confluence of Pretty Hollow Creek and Palmer Creek. The Palmer Creek Trail crosses

Pretty Hollow Creek on a footbridge and then follows Palmer Creek west 3.3 miles to connect with the Balsam Mountain Road.

Continue straight, with the old road now paralleling Pretty Hollow Creek upstream. The trail ascends more steeply as you reach campsite #39 at 1.7 miles on the right. Notice the old rock wall on the left. Just beyond the campsite, you'll see hitching rails and feed stalls for those who have brought horses.

Beyond the camping area the old road fades into a trail as it ascends more steeply up Pretty Hollow Valley. In the ascent to Mt. Sterling Ridge, the trail crosses Pretty Hollow Creek three times and then you must rockhop a small side stream and then Onion Bed Branch. On your way up you'll pass from the cove hardwood forest to the spruce-fir forest of the higher elevations at Pretty Hollow Gap at 5.3 miles.

In the gap, you'll find a junction of trails. Straight ahead, you can take the Swallow Fork Trail down the other side of Mt. Sterling Ridge into the Walnut Bottoms area and connect with the Big Creek Trail. To the left on the Mt. Sterling Ridge Trail, you can walk 4.0 miles to connect with the Balsam Mountain Trail. To the right on the Mt. Sterling Ridge Trail, it's 1.4 miles to a junction with the Mt. Sterling Trail and 0.3 mile farther to the Mt. Sterling firetower and a junction with the Baxter Creek Trail that leads down to the Big Creek Access.

# 52 Little Cataloochee Trail

5.2 miles one way
Moderate
Elevation change: 1000 ft.
Cautions: Creek crossings, muddy sections
Campsites: None
Connections: Pretty Hollow Gap, Long Bunk Trails

**Attractions**: This trail crosses a gap into Little Cataloochee where you'll see remains of the once thriving settlement.

**Trailhead**: Follow the directions in Trail #51 and walk the Pretty Hollow Gap Trail 0.8 mile to the junction on the right with the Little Cataloochee Trail. The other end of the trail is on the dirt road connecting the Cataloochee Access with the Big Creek Access; there's room for a couple of cars there if you want to leave a vehicle for a shuttle. If you are only interested in seeing the old structures remaining in Little Cataloochee, you might want to walk in from this other end and, after you've see enough, retrace your steps back to the place where you parked.

**Description**: As the population grew in Cataloochee, eventually known as "Big Cataloochee," the community spread over the mountain ridge to the north into Little Cataloochee Valley. The first settlers arrived there about 1850. Apple growing became a principal occupation and lasted through the early 1900s.

After walking up the Pretty Hollow Gap Trail to the trail junction, turn right and begin ascending the Little Cataloochee Trail on an old roadbed. In 0.2 mile the trail crosses Little Davidson Branch and then parallels Davidson Branch, headed upstream. You'll cross a small stream and then at 0.7 mile rockhop across Davidson Branch.

As you continue to ascend, notice on the left old fence posts and an open area beyond that was probably once a field. The old roadway fades into a footpath. You'll cross Davidson Branch three more times along with small trickles that feed into it before curving right to follow one branch of the stream up the ridge. At 1.4 miles, the trail is in the creek and you must walk in the shallow water for several yards. The trail ascends more steeply as you continue to climb the ridge. At 1.6 miles you'll pass over a rise with a path to the left that leads to the remains of a log cabin and rock walls below that act as a terrace. The trail descends a short distance from this rise to cross a small stream and then ascends straight up the ridge. Horses that also use this trail have a hard time going straight up and, if there has been a recent rain, will have churned the trail into a quagmire.

You'll top the ridge at Davidson Gap at 2.0 miles and then begin a steep descent with Short Bunk ridge along your left and Noland Mountain along your right, which separates Big Cataloochee from Little Cataloochee. As you descend, you'll begin to notice rock walls. This was the site of the Will Messer Farm, which included the old barn that was relocated to Big Cataloochee and restored in 1977. As you continue to descend, the trail becomes a more obvious road, and at 2.4 miles, you'll pass the ruins of the old Dan Cook place with what's left of the old apple house made of stone on the right. Continue to descend, and you'll pass over Coggins Branch at 2.8 miles. The road crosses Coggins Branch again at 3.0 miles.

You'll then ascend from Coggins Branch to the top of a ridge at 3.2 miles, where you'll find Little Cataloochee Baptist Church, a white frame construction built in 1889 that is still the site of reunions. A cemetery flows down the hill in front of the church. The trail then descends to cross Little Cataloochee Creek on a bridge at 3.7 miles. You'll notice old fence posts and rock walls that are left from the settlement. The road then ascends from the creek to the Hannah Cabin on the left at 4.1 miles; the log house was built about 1864 by John Jackson Hannah.

Continuing up the road, you'll reach a junction with the Long Bunk Trail to the left at 4.2 miles, which leads 3.7 miles north to connect with the Mount Sterling Trail. Continue up the road which at first descends, then goes up and down and crosses a stream on a bridge, to finally ascend in 5.2 miles to connect with old NC284, the dirt road connecting the Cataloochee Access with the Big Creek Access. Big Creek is 9 miles to the left; turning right on the road will return you to Big Cataloochee in 5.5 miles.

194

**Little Cataloochee Baptist Church**

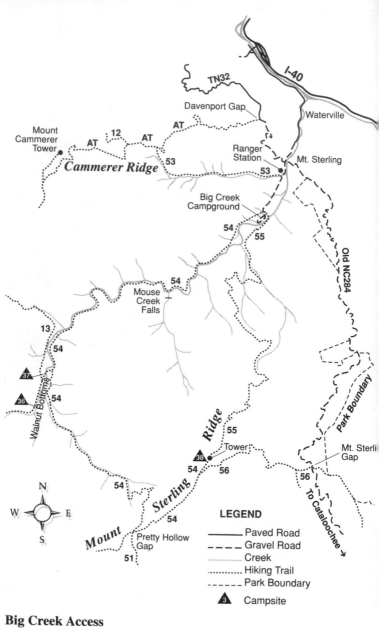

**Big Creek Access**

# 53 Chestnut Branch Trail

2.0 miles one way
(Mt. Cammerer 5.9 miles one way)
Moderate
Elevation gain: 1500 ft. (3300 ft. to Mt. Cammerer)
Cautions: Boggy areas, stream crossings
Campsites: None
Connections: Appalachian Trail

**Attractions**: This pleasant walk along Chestnut Branch provides a shorter route to Mt. Cammerer.

**Trailhead**: To get to the Big Creek Access, drive 60 miles east from Knoxville or 50 miles west from Asheville on I-40 to the Waterville exit. Turn southwest to cross the Pigeon River. On the other side a gravel road heads up the mountain, but bear left to stay on the paved road. You'll cross the Appalachian Trail and circle around and then turn right. You'll soon reach the Walters Plant of the Carolina Power & Light Company. Continue, and the road crosses Big Creek on a small bridge twice and then passes through the Waterville Community. At 1.5 miles from the interstate the road becomes gravel. At 2.2 miles you'll reach an intersection in the community of Mt. Sterling. To the right you can travel a dirt road that at the state line becomes paved TN32 and leads 12 miles to Cosby; so if you are in the Cosby area you can reach the Big Creek Access south along this road. To the left, you can travel a dirt road (old NC284) 16 miles to Cataloochee, and so can come to Big Creek along this road, which is never closed but might have snow and ice in winter. Pass through this intersection and in 0.2 mile farther you'll reach the Big Creek Ranger Station. Park here and walk 50 yards farther down the road. You'll find the trailhead just before the road crosses Chestnut Branch. Turn right on the Chestnut Branch Trail.

**Description**: You'll follow the trail uphill while paralleling Chestnut Branch upstream. The trail at this point is an old

197

roadbed that once led to farming communities up in the hollows. You'll pass through a mixed forest of hemlock, pine, hardwood, and rhododendron.

At about 0.1 mile, the trail begins to get boggy where water runs along the trail before being deflected. On this lower section of the trail, you'll pass through several muddy areas.

The trail levels off where a small stream flows along the right side of the trail, and you'll then begin a gradual climb. As you move into a hardwood forest with small hemlocks, you'll step across a small side stream and at 0.7 mile enter a clearing being taken over by small trees that was once a homesite. You'll see a low rock wall on the right, fragments of tubs, and in spring, blooming daffodils.

The trail then passes close to Chestnut Branch as it reenters a rhododendron woods and climbs above the creek. At 0.9 mile, you'll reach creek level again and begin a steeper climb. The trail switches back right and then left. To your left, watch for views of Mt. Sterling Ridge across Big Creek Valley through the trees.

You'll then walk across a drier south-facing slope with laurel more abundant. The trail then enters a rhododendron thicket. At 1.4 miles the trail crosses a small stream, and then another. You'll cross the same stream again and again and then walk up the stream for a few yards. This is a small water course that may be nonexistent in dry weather.

At 1.6 miles, you'll enter a hollow and follow it up for a short distance, and then bear right to ascend the side of Cammerer Ridge. You'll reach the ridgetop and a junction with the Appalachian Trail at 2.0 miles. To the right, you can reach the Davenport Gap Shelter in 1.0 mile; Davenport Gap itself is 2.0 miles to the right where the AT crosses TN32 at the park boundary.

This is the end of the Chestnut Branch Trail, but turn left on the AT to continue on to Mt. Cammerer. The trail follows along Cammerer Ridge through rhododendron. At 2.5 miles, you'll pass along a drier ridge with laurel, pine, and rhododendron. At 3.0 miles you'll reach a junction with the Lower Mount Cammerer Trail on the right that has ascended 7.4 miles from the Cosby Campground. Continue straight on the AT to get to Mt. Cammerer as described in Trail #12.

198

# 54 Big Creek/Swallow Fork/ Mt. Sterling Ridge Trails

10.4 miles one way
(Mouse Creek Falls 2.0 miles one way)
(Walnut Bottoms 5.0 miles one way)
(Mt. Sterling firetower 10.7 miles one way)
Difficult
Elevation gain: 4100 ft.
Cautions: Steep ascent, mudholes
Campsites: Big Creek Campground, #37, #36, #38
Connections: Low Gap, Camel Gap, Gunter Fork, Pretty
Hollow Gap, Mt. Sterling, Baxter Creek Trails

**Attractions**: This combination of trails is the major segment of one of the best backpacking loops in the park, which takes you to the summit of Mt. Sterling and the Mt. Sterling firetower.

**Trailhead**: Follow the directions in Trail #53 to the Big Creek Ranger Station and continue down the Big Creek Road past the Chestnut Branch Trailhead another 0.7 mile. You'll find the Big Creek Trailhead on the right. Just past the trailhead, you'll see the horse camp on the right, the Group Camp on the left, the tent campground to the right, and a picnic area where you can park.

**Description**: From this parking area you can also pick up the Baxter Creek Trail, which also leads to Mt. Sterling. These trails combine for a 18-mile backpacking loop that's one of the most enjoyable we've found in the park. It's one of those hikes that because of the elevation gain takes you across several climatic zones, like walking north to Canada, from the hardwood coves to the spruce-fir forests at the top of the mountains.

Walk back up the road to the Big Creek Trailhead and begin your hike by passing around boulders that block vehicular passage along an old road. The Big Creek Trail for its entire length follows this once railbed for the logging train of the

**Big Creek**

200

Crestmont Lumber Company. Walnut Bottoms, to which you are headed, was a way station on this rail line.

At 0.1 mile you'll pass a side path on the left that leads down to the campground. The main trail makes a gradual ascent as it passes upstream along Big Creek. The stream spills down among huge grey boulders, which are also scattered uphill to your right. At 1.5 miles watch for stairs on the left that lead down to the streamside next to a forked spillway and a deep, green pool that's great for swimming in summer.

At 2.0 miles, the trail reaches a fenced area on the left with a path that leads to a view across the creek to Mouse Creek Falls, a 40-foot cascade where Mouse Creek drops steeply into Big Creek. Then at 2.4 miles, the trail crosses Big Creek on a bridge.

You'll continue to gradually ascend along the old road to Brakeshoe Springs at 3.0 miles that trickles down the rock wall on your left. Then at 4.3 miles, after a couple of ups and downs, the trail crosses over a side creek and at 4.5 miles passes through Flint Rock Cove Creek on a concrete ford to a junction with the Swallow Fork Trail at 5.0 miles. Turn left here to continue on the loop.

But for camping, continue straight on the Big Creek Trail into Walnut Bottoms, a picturesque setting with hemlocks streamside. The trail crosses Big Creek on a bridge; on the other side is campsite #37. Walnut Bottoms is notorious for bears, so you'll find there a bear-proof locker for food and a tall pole for hanging packs. Just beyond the campsite, you'll find the junction with the Low Gap Trail that leads 2.5 miles up the ridge to the AT on the crest. From there, you can drop into the Cosby Access in another 2.5 miles. Beyond the junction with the Low Gap Trail, is horse camp #36, and then the Big Creek Trail ends and the Camel Gap Trail begins which leads 4.0 miles up to the AT. A half mile along the Camel Gap Trail, you can connect with the Gunter Fork Trail to the left, which leads 4.0 miles to the Balsam Mountain Trail, where you can turn left to the Mt. Sterling Ridge Trail to make an even longer backpacking loop of about 23 miles. Beware that on the Gunter Fork Trail there is no bridge for a crossing of Big Creek, which can be impassable at high water.

Back at the Swallow Fork Trail junction, turn south from the Big Creek Trail and begin a long ascent of Mt. Sterling Ridge. It's this ascent that makes the overall rating difficult. The Swallow Fork Trail is a footpath, but probably still the route of an old road or railbed. The trail crosses two small side streams and then at 5.7 miles parallels Swallow Fork on your right, a tributary of Big Creek.

The trail crosses Swallow Fork on a footbridge at 6.0 miles and continues ascending the ridge. At 6.2 miles, you'll rockhop across McGinty Creek and continue upstream along Swallow Fork to cross a small tributary at 7.0 miles. You'll then leave Swallow Fork and pass upstream along another small tributary and cross it at 7.6 miles. From here up, you'll have a steep climb with a couple of switchbacks to Pretty Hollow Gap in the spruce-fir zone on Mt. Sterling Ridge at 9.0 miles.

Pretty Hollow Gap is indeed pretty, with grassy areas and in spring an expanse of spring beauties. In the gap, you'll find a junction. The Pretty Hollow Gap Trail is straight ahead and leads down the other side of the ridge into Cataloochee Valley. To the right, the Mt. Sterling Ridge Trail leads 4.0 miles to the Balsam Mountain Trail. To keep on the loop described here, turn left on the Mt. Sterling Ridge Trail headed for the Mt. Sterling firetower.

The trail follows Mt. Sterling Ridge as it leads to the summit of Mt. Sterling. Through the trees to both sides you can occasionally see the surrounding mountains and valleys. The trail is steep in places, and you'll have to walk through or around mudholes created by the horses that also use this trail, but it's a good walk through the spruce-fir forest, dark and cool. At 10.4 miles, you'll reach an open, grassy area and a junction with the Mt. Sterling Trail to the right, which is a jeep road that has climbed from old NC284.

Continue straight on the jeep road another 0.3 mile to the summit of Mt. Sterling where you'll find campsite #38 and the Mt. Sterling firetower. The views are some of the best in the park, with Mt. Cammerer to the north. Since the park does not maintain the tower for observation purposes, we do not recommend that you climb the stairs. At the Mt. Sterling firetower, you'll connect with the Baxter Creek Trail, which leads 6.2 miles down to Big Creek. Or if you have a car waiting for you on old NC284, you can walk down the Mt. Sterling Trail.

# 55 Baxter Creek Trail

6.2 miles one way
Difficult
Elevation gain: 4100 ft.
Cautions: Steep ascent, stream crossings
Campsites: Big Creek Campground, #38
Connections: Big Creek, Mt. Sterling Ridge,
Mt. Sterling Trails

**Attractions**: This is one of the prettiest trails in the park as it climbs from the cove hardwood forest through the spruce-fir forest of the higher elevations to the Mt. Sterling firetower; it also serves as the final leg of one of the best loop backpacks.

**Trailhead**: Follow the directions in Trail #54 to the Big Creek picnic area.

**Description**: The Baxter Creek Trail is a shorter walk to the summit of Mt. Sterling than the Big Creek/Swallow Fork/Mt. Sterling Ridge walk and it combines with these trails to make a great 18-mile backpacking loop. The Big Creek Trail begins at this same location just back up the road.

To walk to Mt. Sterling on the Baxter Creek Trail, begin at the picnic area by crossing Big Creek on a bridge. You'll then turn right, following Big Creek upstream. At 0.2 mile, Big Creek swings away from you, but you will continue to hear it for a time. As the trail approaches Baxter Creek as it flows down Mt. Sterling Ridge to join Big Creek, the trail curves left to begin a relentless climb to the summit of Mt. Sterling.

In spring, the trail is lined with blooming crested dwarf iris. At 0.7 mile, you'll rockhop across Baxter Creek and continue ascending upstream. You'll see an occasional large poplar and at 0.8 mile an unusual hemlock on the right that has branched into half a dozen trunks.

The trail crosses a small stream and at 1.3 miles curves away from Baxter Creek to the right. Notice through this curve the

203

white-blooming stonecrop growing on almost every rock and boulder in sight. At 1.7 miles, you'll rockhop across a tributary of Baxter Creek.

At 2.6 miles the trail passes a huge chestnut snag on the right and then through thick rhododendron. You'll see a large hemlock on the left at 2.8 miles. This next section of trail ascends through a mature forest of hemlocks, at first with hardwoods intermingled—part of the virgin woods that were acquired for the park before they were cut for lumber and pulpwood. At 3.0 miles, you must climb over a large hemlock lying across the trail, unless it has been removed by the time you reach this spot. The large trees reach into the higher elevations until at about 3.9 miles, you begin to see large spruce trees intermingled with the hemlock. Eventually the hemlock give way to the large spruce. At 4.3 miles watch for an oak on the left that has a huge burl.

The trail now ascends completely in the spruce-fir forest, cool and dark and silent. At 4.4 miles the trail reaches Mt. Sterling Ridge and makes a switchback right. At one time, you could pick up the Big Branch Trail to the left that also led up from the Big Creek picnic area, but the trail has been long abandoned. From this switchback, the Baxter Creek Trail climbs along Mt. Sterling Ridge as it leads to the summit of Mt. Sterling. This may be the prettiest part of the trail. The Baxter Creek Trail is strictly a hiking trail where horses have not trampled the vegetation and churned the trail to mudholes. So it's just a path through the woods, a path lined with fern and Clinton's lily that passes among gray boulders draped in moss amid a dense spruce-fir forest gently humming with a cool breeze.

Just before the summit, at 5.9 miles, a side trail leads to your right to a water source for those that are spending the night on the mountain. At 6.2 miles, you'll reach the end of the Baxter Creek Trail as you emerge into a clearing where the firetower crowns the summit. To your right, you'll find campsite #38.

Straight, the trail leads down an old road to a junction with the Mt. Sterling Trail headed left down the ridge to old NC284 and the Mt. Sterling Ridge Trail continuing straight down the ridge to Pretty Hollow Gap.

**Mt. Sterling Tower**

# 56 Mount Sterling Trail

2.3 miles one way
(Mt. Sterling firetower 2.6 miles one way)
Moderate
Elevation gain: 1860 ft.
Cautions: Steady ascent, rocky sections
Campsites: #38
Connections: Asbury, Long Bunk, Mt. Sterling Ridge Trails

**Attractions**: This trail provides a short route to the top of Mt. Sterling.

**Trailhead**: Follow the directions in Trail #53 to the road intersection in the Mt. Sterling community. Turn left toward Cataloochee. This is old NC284, a one-lane gravel road for much of its length, but not one way. It's easily negotiated by cars but can be a little jarring. At one mile, the road forks; stay to the right. Keep straight and you'll enter the park at 4 miles. Then at 6.6 miles, you'll find the trailhead on the right. There's room to park along the road.

**Description**: You'll also find at this trailhead the Asbury Trail that leads to the left to reconnect with old NC284 at about 4 miles along the road and then drops off to cross Cataloochee Creek at Asbury Crossing. The trail then follows the boundary of the park to connect with the road again at about 10 miles along the road. The trail was once part of the Cherokee trail system through the Great Smokies. It is called the "Asbury Trail" because it was the route followed by Bishop Francis Asbury, the "horse-back apostle of Methodism" who carried his doctrine throughout the mountains around 1800.

Begin the Mt. Sterling Trail to the right. You'll pass around a gate and begin ascending immediately in a mixed hardwood forest. You'll find little relief from the steady ascent as the trail climbs Mt. Sterling Ridge. For its entire length, the trail follows a jeep road, which is now also a horse trail.

Watch for a large oak on the right after about 0.1 mile. The trail then begins to parallel a powerline that runs up to the tower atop Mt. Sterling, which is used for a radio repeater. For a short stretch at about 0.2 mile, you can see directly up the mountain to the firetower.

At 0.5 mile, you'll reach a junction with the Long Bunk Trail, which leads left 3.7 miles to connect with the Little Cataloochee Trail. Stay straight on the Mt. Sterling Trail, and you'll soon switchback right and at 1.0 mile enter a hemlock woods. Then at 1.2 miles you'll climb into the cooler spruce-fir zone of the mountain's forest. At about 1.4 miles, the trail climbs along a drier south-facing slope of laurel and pine but soon reenters the spruce-fir-rhododendron woods. At 1.8 miles, you'll cross under the powerline as you see it for the last time along the trail.

At 2.0 miles, you'll cross through a more open section and pass a small spring that in wet weather washes the trail. You'll then climb more steeply. Then at 2.3 miles, you'll reach the crest of Mt. Sterling Ridge and the junction with the Mt. Sterling Ridge Trail. The junction lies in an open grassy area that is great for laying out lunch and soaking up the sun.

The Mt. Sterling Ridge Trail leads left to connect with the Pretty Hollow Gap and Swallow Fork Trails in Pretty Hollow Gap and beyond, the Balsam Mountain Trail. Turn right to get to the Mt. Sterling Tower in about 0.3 mile. You'll also find there campsite #38 and the beginning of the Baxter Creek Trail.

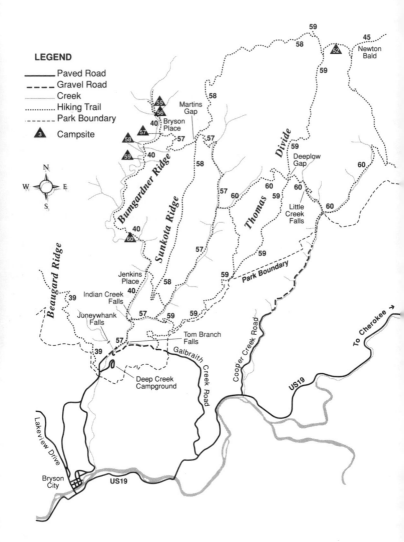

LEGEND

———— Paved Road
‑ ‑ ‑ Gravel Road
——— Creek
········· Hiking Trail
– – – Park Boundary

▲3 Campsite

N
W — E
S

Newton
Bald 45

59
58
▲52
59

▲55
▲56
Martins
Gap
58

40
Bryson
Place
▲58 ▲57
57 57

Deeplow
Gap
59

Little
Creek
Falls
60

▲59
40

Bumgardner Ridge

58

57 60

60 60
59

Thomas Divide

60

▲40
▲60

57

59

Sunkota Ridge

Jenkins
Place
40

58

Indian Creek
Falls

59

Juneywhank
Falls

57

59

59

Park Boundary

Beaugard Ridge

39

57

Tom Branch
Falls

39

Galbraith Creek Road

Cooper Creek Road

To Cherokee →

Deep Creek
Campground

US19

Lakeview Drive

Bryson
City

US19

**Deep Creek Access**

208

# 57 Indian Creek/Martins Gap Trails

7.2 miles one way
(Tom Branch Falls 0.2 mile one way)
(Indian Creek Falls 0.7 mile one way)
Moderate
Elevation change: 1600 ft.
Cautions: Mudholes on the Martins Gap Section
Campsites: Deep Creek Campground, #57
Connections: Deep Creek, Stone Pile Gap, Loop,
Deeplow Gap, Sunkota Ridge Trails

**Attractions**: This hike offers an easy walk past two waterfalls and in spring grand wildflower displays before leaving the graded road to climb Sunkota Ridge.

**Trailhead**: From the Oconaluftee Visitor Center on Newfound Gap Road, head south into the town of Cherokee. In 3.5 miles, turn right on US19. In another 10 miles you'll reach Bryson City, where you'll turn right on Everett Street to cross the Tuckasegee River and pass through town. (If you are coming from Fontana, take NC28 east to US74 and then to Bryson City.) In town you'll see a sign directing a right turn on Depot Street toward the Deep Creek Access, but for an easier route, keep straight and just out of town take the right turn at another sign directing you toward Deep Creek. After making the turn, you'll immediately turn left and then make another left after driving 1.4 miles. In another half mile, you'll enter the park. Continue into the Deep Creek area past the ranger station and the campground to where the road is gated.

**Description**: Deep Creek is the area in which the ancient Cherokee town of Kituhwa was located, perhaps the first Chero- kee village. The Cherokees, in addition to calling themselves the Principal People, were known as the "Ani-Kituhwagi," the people of Kituhwa.

209

**Tom Branch Falls**

At the Deep Creek Trailhead, begin your walk around the gate and up the gravel road that ascends upstream along Deep Creek. In just 0.2 mile you'll see Tom Branch Falls cascading down 50 feet to join Deep Creek on the other side. As you continue up Deep Creek, you'll cross the creek on a bridge at 0.3 mile and begin a steeper climb along the old road. Watch for wildflower displays in spring—wild geranium, phlox, rue anemone, trillium, bishop's cap, foam flower, toothwort, showy orchis, and the flowering trees, dogwood and silverbell. In summer, you'll see people riding inner tubes in the creek, for this is a favorite stretch for tubing.

At 0.7 mile, you'll reach a junction with the Deep Creek Trail continuing north on an old roadbed, eventually topping out on Newfound Gap Road in 13.2 miles. Turn right to continue on the Indian Creek Trail, which is also an old road; these roads were left from a planned Indian Creek Motor Nature Trail that was to follow Indian Creek; some work was done in the 1970s, but objections to building roads in the park caused the project to be abandoned.

In just 200 feet after the turn, you'll reach a side path on the left that drops down to Indian Creek Falls, a broad cascade of 60 feet on Indian Creek. As the trail continues to climb from the waterfall, you'll cross Indian Creek on a bridge and then remain on the creek's left. At 1.2 miles, the Stone Pile Gap Trail leaves on the right to drop to a footbridge crossing of Indian Creek and to connect with the Thomas Divide Trail in one mile. As you continue your gradual ascent from this junction, watch for long stretches of blooming crested dwarf iris in late April. At 1.5 miles, you'll reach a junction with the one-mile Loop Trail to the left that forms a 3.7-mile loop with the Indian Creek and Deep Creek Trails; this makes a good dayhike. Keep straight on the Indian Creek Trail which continues to ascend on the old road while paralleling the cascading Indian Creek upstream. At 2.2 miles, you'll see a path to the left that leads up to the Laney Cemetery.

You'll cross Indian Creek on road bridges at 2.9 miles and 3.4 miles. Just before making the second crossing, you'll see a side trail that leads up to the old Queen Cemetery. Continuing straight, you'll make one more crossing of Indian Creek on a

**Indian Creek Falls**

bridge just before reaching a junction with the Deeplow Gap Trail on the right at 3.7 miles. Continue straight on the old road, making a gradual ascent while still following Indian Creek upstream. The road crosses Indian Creek once again on a bridge at 3.9 miles. You'll pass more spreads of crested dwarf iris and cross Indian Creek on a bridge again at 4.2 miles. The road then passes over Estes Branch and reaches a turnaround at the end of the road at 4.3 miles. This is also the end of the Indian Creek Trail. At the upper part of the turnaround loop, you'll find the beginning of the Martins Gap Trail, which turns off to the left to continue the walk.

The Martins Gap Trail is a footpath that is also a horse trail; you'll find a few mudholes along the way. At 4.5 miles, you'll cross Indian Creek twice on footbridges as you continue ascending upstream. The trail crosses Indian Creek on a footbridge for the last time at 4.9 miles. You'll then begin your ascent of Sunkota Ridge with a switchback left.

The trail passes through a muddy area where a trickle has wet the trail. You'll ascend through a mixed forest of hardwood, hemlock, rhododendron, and laurel as you make two more switchbacks. You'll then follow a small stream on your right to the head of a cove where you'll make a switchback left onto an old roadbed to complete your ascent to Martins Gap at the top of Sunkota Ridge at 5.7 miles. In the gap, the trail intersects with the Sunkota Ridge Trail, which leads right 4.9 miles to connect with the Thomas Divide Trail and left 3.8 miles to connect with the Loop Trail.

The Martins Gap Trail continues straight, descending the west side of Sunkota Ridge to connect with the Deep Creek Trail at 7.2 miles at Bryson Place and campsite #57.

# 58 Sunkota Ridge Trail

8.7 miles one way
Moderate
Elevation gain: 2400 ft.
Cautions: Overgrown in places
Campsites: None
Connections: Loop, Martins Gap, Thomas Divide Trails

**Attractions**: This trail connects trails out of Deep Creek.

**Trailhead**: Follow the directions in Trail #57 to the gate on the Deep Creek Road and then hike up the Indian Creek Trail 1.5 miles and turn left on the Loop Trail to ascend another half mile to the top of Sunkota Ridge and the beginning of the trail.

**Description**: From the Loop Trail, you'll ascend along Sunkota Ridge, continually climbing while occasionally passing over small knolls. This is a seldom used trail, so you might find it a little overgrown in places even though it is also a horse trail. When we hiked the trail last, there were a number of trees down across the trail that we had to duck under or crawl over.

The trail climbs through a mixed hardwood forest. You'll pass through thickets of laurel and rhododendron and at 1.7 miles reach a small gap where the trail switches left to continue up the ridge. The trail ascends up a knoll at 3.2 miles, and then drops and passes over a smaller knoll to descend to Martins Gap at 3.8 miles and an intersection with the Martins Gap Trail.

The Sunkota Ridge Trail can be used to make loop hikes in the Deep Creek area. A walk up the Indian Creek and Martins Gap Trails to Martins Gap and then down the Sunkota Ridge Trail and back to the Deep Creek Trailhead makes a loop of around 11 miles. A walk up the Deep Creek Trail to Bryson Place and east on the Martins Gap Trail to Martins Gap and then down the Sunkota Ridge Trail and back to the Deep Creek Trailhead makes a loop of about 13 miles. The Sunkota Ridge Trail itself continues north, ascending to the Thomas Divide Trail at 8.7 miles.

# 🔢 Stone Pile Gap/Thomas Divide Trails

13.9 miles one way
(Deeplow Gap 5.4 miles one way)
Elevation gain: 2600 ft.
Moderate
Cautions: Creek crossings, overgrown in places
Campsites: #52
Connections: Indian Creek, Deeplow Gap, Newton Bald,
Sunkota Ridge, Kanati Fork Trails

**Attractions**: This trail leads along Thomas Ridge from Deep Creek to the Newfound Gap Road, providing several connections for loop hikes.

**Trailhead**: Follow the directions in Trail #57 to the gate on the Deep Creek Road and then walk up the Indian Creek Trail 1.2 miles to the beginning of the Stone Pile Gap Trail.

**Description**: The Stone Pile Gap Trail acts as a connector from the Indian Creek Trail to the Thomas Divide Trail. After turning right on the Stone Pile Gap Trail, you'll drop down to a footbridge crossing of Indian Creek. The trail passes through a rhododendron bottomland and then begins the climb up Thomas Ridge. The climb is steep in places, and you'll make several small stream crossings before topping the ridge at 1.0 mile to connect with the Thomas Divide Trail.

This southern end of the Thomas Divide Trail is an old road bed that was part of the Indian Creek Motor Nature Trail. You can walk 1.1 miles to the right to connect with the Galbraith Creek Road, which runs from near the end of the Deep Creek Road east to US19 between Bryson City and Cherokee. The connection with the Thomas Divide Trail is 1.2 miles east along the road from Deep Creek; you'll see on the left a jeep road blocked by a gate. You can begin the Thomas Divide Trail there. But because there is very little parking space, the more popular way to begin the Thomas Divide Trail is up the Indian Creek and Stone Pile Gap Trails as we describe here.

From the junction with the Stone Pile Gap Trail, turn north and walk up the old roadbed, ascending along Thomas Ridge. You'll find the road occasionally overgrown since this is now a seldom used trail. After a continuous moderate ascent, you'll reach at 3.0 miles a junction with two options. Straight ahead you can stay on the old roadbed 2.0 miles to connect with the Deeplow Gap Trail and then the Indian Creek Trail; this was to be the route of the motor nature trail. But to stay on the Thomas Divide Trail, turn right off the road onto a footpath; you'll almost immediately turn left and continue your ascent of Thomas Ridge.

Again you'll find places overgrown beginning in late spring, heavy with poison ivy but also at around 3.8 miles one of the largest displays of wild geranium in the park; spring blooms of pink to purple cover the slopes. The trail ascends and descends as it passes over knolls on Thomas Ridge while gradually gaining in elevation. At 4.3 miles, you'll top a last knoll to then make a long descent to Deeplow Gap, which is just that, deep and low, at 5.4 miles. Here you'll find the Deeplow Gap Trail that leads left to connect with the Indian Creek Trail for a loop hike back to the Deep Creek access and right to connect with the Mingus Creek Trail that leads to Newton Bald.

From Deeplow Gap, the Thomas Divide Trail continues north up Thomas Ridge. At 8.5 miles you'll reach a junction with the Newton Bald Trail leading right 0.5 mile to a junction with the Mingus Creek Trail and Newton Bald.

Continue straight on the Thomas Divide Trail for another half mile to a junction with the Sunkota Ridge Trail to the left, which leads 4.9 miles down Sunkota Ridge to Martins Gap and then on down the ridge into the Deep Creek area, connecting with the Loop Trail.

Continuing north on the Thomas Divide Trail, you'll reach the junction with the Kanati Fork Trail at 12.2 miles and finally Newfound Gap Road at 13.9 miles.

# 60 Deeplow Gap Trail

6.0 miles one way
(Little Creek Falls 3.0 miles one way)
Moderate
Cautions: Creek crossings
Campsites: None
Connections: Indian Creek, Thomas Divide,
Mingus Creek Trails

**Attractions**: This trail connects several trails for loop routes and takes you by a long cascade on Little Creek.

**Trailhead**: Follow the directions in Trail #57 to the gate on the Deep Creek Road and walk up the Indian Creek Trail 3.7 miles to the beginning of the Deeplow Gap Trail on the right.

**Description**: Turning right on the Deeplow Gap Trail off the Indian Creek Trail, you'll ascend along an old roadway that was part of the proposed Indian Creek Motor Nature Trail. At 0.1 mile the road crosses over Georges Branch on a bridge. Continue ascending up the roadway until at 0.3 mile you'll see a path to the left that is the continuation of the Deeplow Gap Trail; a sign points the way to Thomas Divide. The roadway continues straight to also connect with the Thomas Divide Trail in 2.0 miles.

Turn left on the footpath that follows an even older roadway and begin your ascent of Thomas Ridge. You'll cross several small streams and trickles as you ascend through a hardwood forest with ferns and iris along the trail. At 1.1 miles the old roadbed fades into a pathway. Beyond, you'll climb into a hemlock woods that has several large trees.

At 1.9 miles, the trail makes a hairpin turn right and ascends to Deeplow Gap on Thomas Ridge at 2.3 miles. Here the trail intersects with the Thomas Divide Trail that leads right 5.4 miles back to the Deep Creek area and left toward Newton Bald and the Newfound Gap Road.

**Little Creek Falls**

218

Stay straight to descend the other side of the ridge on the Deeplow Gap Trail. You'll descend steeply with switchbacks and rockhop across Little Creek at 2.7 miles. You'll then cross a smaller tributary and descend downstream along Little Creek, which is covered at this point in leucothoe, or dog hobble. At 2.8 miles, you'll be able to see the top of Little Creek Falls on your right. Continue down the trail to a switchback right at 2.9 miles and then descend to the bottom of Little Creek Falls at 3.0 miles, a beautiful cascade of 40 feet or more, depending on where you designate the top and bottom.

The trail crosses Little Creek on a log right at the foot of the cascade and continues to descend from the falls. This stretch is good for wildflowers in spring. You'll make a switchback left to cross Little Creek again and then cross a side stream to eventually bottom out at Cooper Creek at 3.8 miles. At a junction here, an old roadway leads right following in and out of Cooper Creek to the Cooper Creek Road off US19 at Ela. This is not a recommended access because the road gets rough and you must park on private property, but if you do use this access, be sure to ask for permission at the nearby trout farm. To the left at this junction, the Deeplow Gap Trail, this section sometimes called the "Cooper Creek Trail," leads up the ridge to connect with the Mingus Creek Trail at 6.0 miles; a currently unmaintained section drops down to Mingus Mill on the Newfound Gap Road and a still used section leads along the ridgeline to Newton Bald.

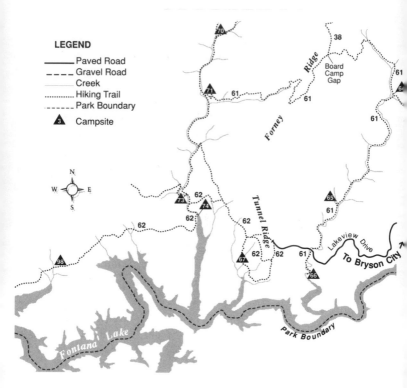

## LEGEND

——— Paved Road
– – – Gravel Road
——— Creek
·········· Hiking Trail
· – · – · – Park Boundary
▲ 3 Campsite

**Lakeview Drive Access**

220

# ⑥1 Noland Creek/Springhouse Branch Trails

11.7 miles
Moderate
Elevation change: 2200 ft.
Cautions: Creek crossings
Campsites: #65, #64, #71
Connections: Noland Divide, Forney Ridge,
Forney Creek Trails

**Attractions**: This combination of trails is part of a good back-packing loop connecting Noland Creek with Forney Creek.

**Trailhead**: From Bryson City, head north on Everett Street toward Deep Creek. But instead of making the turn to Deep Creek Campground just north of town, continue straight on the highway, which winds around and becomes Lakeview Drive. At 3 miles from Bryson City, you'll enter the park, and in another 5 miles, you'll find the Noland Creek Trailhead parking on the left.

**Description**: When the Tennessee Valley Authority built its Fontana Dam on the Little Tennessee River in the early 1940s, old NC288 that was along the north bank of the river was flooded. TVA would have rebuilt the road above the lake waters, but since this was during World War II, the resources were not available. Instead TVA, in what has since been termed the "1943 agreement," bought the 44,000 acres that are north of the lake and south of what was then the park boundary and turned the land over to the Department of Interior to be included in the park, with Interior to rebuild the Northshore Road sometime in the future.

The National Park Service actually started the road through the park lands, which now run down to the lakeshore, and completed 5.6 miles by 1968 before it was decided the road was not really necessary. This completed section of the Northshore Road is now the Lakeview Drive that you use to reach the Noland Creek Trailhead. Although the Northshore Road will surely never be completed, the road remains an obstacle to park preservation. Those in North Carolina who still holdout for some compensation from the 1943 agreement have so far effectively blocked wilderness designation for the park.

Begin by walking around the gate and down the paved road to the left of the parking area. After a steep descent, you'll intersect with the Noland Creek Trail. To the left the trail crosses Noland Creek on a bridge and leads 1 mile toward Fontana Lake to campsite #66 where it deadends. Turn right to head north on the Noland Creek Trail, paralleling Noland Creek upstream.

In 0.2 mile you'll pass under the Lakeview Drive bridge and then cross Noland Creek on a bridge. You'll continue ascending along the old roadway until at 1.8 miles the road curves right and a side trail to the left leads up to campsite #65 along Bearpen Branch, which flows under the road at this junction.

Continue up the road; two more streams flow under the road. At 2.4 miles watch for a good lunch spot where the creek flows through large slabs of rock in the creekbed. You'll pass through a pine forest and cross Noland Creek on a bridge at 2.5 miles.

The road continues to climb, sometimes steeply, until you cross Noland Creek on a bridge again at 3.2 miles. Just across the bridge an old jeep trail leads left, but stay with the main road as it curves right. You'll cross Noland Creek on a bridge again at 4.5 miles and then again at 4.7 miles and reach a junction with the Springhouse Branch Trail in an area called "Solola Valley" that was populated before the days of the park establishment. Here is also campsite #64.

From this junction, the Noland Creek Trail continues straight up the old roadway 4.8 miles to connect with the Noland Divide Trail at Sassafras Gap, along the way crossing Noland Creek several times and passing campsites #63, #62, and #61. Turn left on the Springhouse Branch Trail. You'll pass through the campsite and walk up a footpath that for a few yards joins Mill Creek where you walk in shallow water. You'll then leave the creek and ascend along an old roadbed. You'll pass an old homesite on the left with piles of rock and then at 5.3 miles cross Mill Creek on a footbridge with the railing half fallen down. The trail then passes through a once-settled area with rock walls, rusted wash basins, and remains of a chimney.

222

The trail ascends into a hemlock woods and through a large carpet of groundpine, following Springhouse Branch upstream. At 6.0 miles, you'll curve left to rockhop a stream and cross several small branches that converge to make Springhouse Branch. At 6.7 miles, the trail tops a ridge leading down from Forney Ridge and curves right to climb along the ridgeline.

The trail follows the left side of the ridge and enters a rhododendron thicket to cross two shallow streams and then swing through a cove. You'll then descend to Board Camp Gap along the ridgeline of Forney Ridge at 7.7 miles and a junction. The Forney Ridge Trail leads right 3.6 miles to the Forney Ridge Parking Area at the end of the Clingmans Dome Road.

Continue straight to stay on the Springhouse Branch Trail that now climbs from the gap to follow Forney Ridge before curving right at 8.2 miles and descending. The trail then ascends again and then descends to a gap at 8.9 miles where you'll switchback right and descend off the ridge. At 9.4 miles, you'll cross Bee Gum Branch and then descend while paralleling Bee Gum Branch downstream. At 9.8 miles, a spring joins the trail.

You'll curve right at 10.0 miles to a dry slope that affords views through the trees of Forney Creek Valley. The trail continues to descend passing in and out of coves. At 11.5 miles you'll switchback left and then switchback right to descend to a small stream crossing and a junction with the Forney Creek Trail at 11.7 miles, where you'll find campsite #71. In the campsite, you'll see a large intact chimney and a bathtub left over from the days when this was a CCC camp.

The Forney Creek Trail leads right from this trail junction 8 miles to connect with the Forney Ridge Trail. A good 18-mile backpack hike heads down the Forney Ridge Trail and then loops back using the Springhouse Branch and Forney Creek Trails.

Left from the junction with the Springhouse Branch Trail, the Forney Creek Trail follows the east side of Forney Creek 3 miles to end at the Forney Creek embayment on Fontana Lake. To loop back to Lakeview Drive, take the White Oak Branch Trail, which is 1.0 mile down the Forney Creek Trail to the left. This trail in 2 miles joins the Lakeshore Trail that connects with the Tunnel Trail and the road. Including your walk down the road to return to the Noland Creek Trailhead, the loop hike is 17.5 miles.

**Tunnel Trail**

# 🖉 Lakeshore Trail

25.2 miles one way
Moderate
Elevation change: 600 ft.
Cautions: Creek crossings, overgrown in places
Campsites: #74, #98, #75, #76, #77, #81, #86
Connections: Goldmine Loop, Tunnel, Forney Creek,
Hazel Creek Trails

**Attractions**: This long trail follows along Fontana Lake, which is the reservoir behind Fontana Dam.

**Trailhead**: Follow the directions in Trail #61 along Lakeview Drive out of Bryson City past the Noland Creek Trailhead and continue to where the road is gated. Just before the gate on the road, you'll see the beginning of the Lakeshore Trail on the left. Parking is on the right. At the end of the road is the beginning of the 0.7-mile Tunnel Trail that you can use to connect with the Lakeshore Trail and save 1.4 miles of walking. If you take that route you'll soon encounter the tunnel that was to be part of the Northshore Road that has since been abandoned. The trail follows the road right into the tunnel that extends for about 200 yards. By the time you get to the center it will be quite dark, although you still can see the light from both ends since the tunnel is straight. After the tunnel you'll reach the end of the pavement and beyond, the Lakeshore Trail.

**Description**: Begin at the Lakeshore Trailhead on your left just before the end of the road. You'll begin your walk in a hemlock and hardwood forest thick with rhododendron. The trail is at first level, but then ascends moderately through carpets of ferns. You'll reach a gap at 0.3 mile with faint trails heading both left and right, but keep straight to stay on the Lakeshore Trail. The trail then passes along the slope of a ridge to reach the top at a junction at 0.5 mile with the Goldmine Loop Trail that leads left toward Fontana Lake before turning back to the Lakeshore Trail.

225

Continue on the Lakeshore Trail by curving to the right at this junction. The trail passes along the side of the ridge into an open area on a dry slope at 1.6 miles. Streams wet the trail at 1.8 miles. From here, you'll climb to the point of a ridgeline at 2.1 miles and a junction with the Tunnel Trail to the right that leads back to the road. You can use this route for a short loop hike.

Turn left to stay on the Lakeshore Trail. You'll round the point and at 2.2 miles reach a junction with the other end of the Goldmine Loop Trail on the left.

Stay straight on the Lakeshore Trail to curve around another point to the right and then wind along the slope of the ridge, passing through coves with small streams and trickles of water. At 2.8 miles, the trail passes up a cove and then climbs out of it to the right and passes over the ridge. You'll descend the other side to a shallow creek crossing at 3.2 miles. The trail continues to descend to a junction at 3.6 miles with the White Oak Branch Trail that leads up an old roadbed to the right over a gap and descends to White Oak Branch and a junction with the Forney Creek Trail in 2.0 miles.

Bear left to stay on the Lakeshore Trail. You'll descend to a clearing with a pile of stones on the right that must have been a housesite. At 3.7 miles, the trail crosses the shallow stream you crossed above. You'll now be descending along an old roadbed that once led to the old housesite. At a fork in the road, turn to the right. The trail now follows this road down to an old log bridge over a small stream at 3.8 miles. The road then forks again; turn left. The trail climbs to pass around a point and descend to cross a small stream at 4.3 miles. You'll then climb to round another point where you can hear Forney Creek below and then descend to a junction with the Forney Creek Trail on an old road beside Forney Creek at 4.7 miles.

To the right, the Forney Creek Trail leads up toward Clingmans Dome. A half mile along the trail, you'll pass a junction with the Bear Creek Trail that leads left to cross Forney Creek on a bridge, where you'll find campsite #73, and then ascends along Bear Creek and Jumpup Ridge to connect in 5.8 miles with the Welch Ridge Trail just east of High Rocks along Welch Ridge, named for the Welch family, early settlers of the Forney Creek Valley. The path is steep, from which Jumpup

Ridge gets its name; this was once called the "Jumpup Ridge Trail." Farther up the Forney Creek Trail, you can reach the Springhouse Branch and Jonas Creek Trails.

The Lakeshore Trail follows the Forney Creek Trail to the left. Turn and walk down the roadbed while paralleling Forney Creek to the right. You'll cross Forney Creek on a bridge at 4.8 miles and then reach campsite #74 on the Forney Creek embayment of Fontana Lake at 4.9 miles. The road continues straight into the water, while the Lakeshore Trail turns right to traverse the edge of the embayment.

The Lakeshore Trail continues to follow along the north shore of Fontana Lake for the next 20.3 miles, with no trail connections, to Hazel Creek at the old community of Proctor. Along the way, you can spend the night at campsites #98, #75, #76, #77, and #81; campsites #77 and #81 are new sites that are scheduled to be opened the winter of 1991-92. You'll find campsite #86 on the Hazel Creek embayment at Proctor. The site of the old lumber town, where a few structures remain, is now completely cutoff from the outside world except for trail connections or a boat ride across Fontana Lake.

At Proctor, the Lakeshore Trail connects with the Hazel Creek Trail that leads to the northeast, eventually connecting with the Welch Ridge Trail below Silers Bald on the Smokies crest. Plans for the Lakeshore Trail call for eventually extending the trail farther west along the lakeshore to connect with another completed section out of the Fontana Dam Access. For now, to get to that other section, you must walk 4.5 miles up the Hazel Creek Trail, then 2.5 miles west on the Sugar Fork Trail to a junction with the Jenkins Ridge Trail and the Pinnacle Creek Trail, then continue west 3.5 miles on the Pinnacle Creek Trail, and then down the Eagle Creek Trail where you can pick up the other section of the Lakeshore Trail, described in Trail #63.

**LEGEND**

───── Paved Road

━ ━ ━ Gravel Road

───── Creek

············· Hiking Trail

─·─·─· Park Boundary

🔺③ Campsite

**Twentymile/Fontana Dam Access**

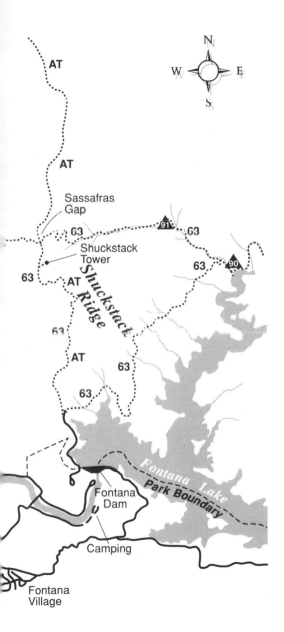

 **Shuckstack Loop**

13.0 miles  - 15.2
(Shuckstack firetower 3.7 miles one way)
Difficult
Elevation change: 2100 ft.
Cautions: Creek fords, steep ascents
Campsites: #90, #91
Connections: Eagle Creek, Appalachian Trails

**Attractions**: This combination of a 5.5-mile section of the Lakeshore Trail, the 3.5-mile Lost Cove Trail, and a 4.0-mile piece of the AT makes a good backpack loop that takes you by the Shuckstack firetower for incredible views.

**Trailhead**: Coming from the Deep Creek Access, take US19 west out of Bryson City. At 3.5 miles you'll join US74; at 5.7 miles NC28 joins US19/74 on the left. Turn right on NC28 at 8.8 miles when it separates from US19/74. At 30.5 miles, you'll come to a "T" with the Fontana Dam Access to the right. Or if you're coming from the Abrams Creek Access, head southeast on US129. You'll pass the Parson Branch Road exit from Cades Cove in 10.4 miles, and then at 15.1 miles turn left on NC28. The Twentymile Access is on the left at 18.0 miles. Continue, and at 23.1 miles you'll pass the turnoff on the left for the bottom of Fontana Dam. Stay on the highway up the hill, pass Fontana Village on the right, and you'll reach the turnoff for the top of the dam at 25 miles where NC28 makes a right-angle turn to the right. Coming from either direction, now take the road in to the top of the Fontana Dam. You'll cross over the dam at 1.2 miles and on the other side turn right to the end of the road at 2.3 miles.

**Description**: In the early 1940s, aluminum was needed for America's airplanes in World War II. The process to produce aluminum requires great amounts of electricity. So in 1941, the federal government proposed building a dam on the Little Tennessee River to supply the needed electric power to produce aluminum at ALCOA's nearby plant in southeast Tennessee. From 1942 till 1945, the Tennessee Valley Authority, a federal agency, constructed the 480-foot-high Fontana Dam, which is still in operation. To house the workers, TVA constructed the community of Fontana that is today a resort village in these remote mountains of eastern North Carolina. The Fontana name came from a nearby lumber mill town.

At the end of the road, after crossing over Fontana Dam, you'll see that the Lakeshore Trail begins straight ahead while the Appalachian Trail emerges on the left to leave the park by continuing south back across Fontana Dam and into the Nantahala National Forest. For a dayhike, you can walk up the AT to the Shuckstack firetower, a steep 3.7-mile climb, and then return. But to do the entire loop, head straight on the Lakeshore Trail. Step over the cable and walk down the road, which is slowly being taken over by grass. At 0.1 mile you'll reach the end of the road and descend into a cove of pine and hardwood. You'll see through the trees the waters of Fontana Lake. At 0.7 mile the trail turns up along a stream a few yards to a rockhop crossing. From here the trail ascends to a gap at 1.0 mile and then descends the other side, following a small stream into a hemlock cove.

You'll find remains of an old car at 1.3 miles and then an open grassy area with another skeleton of a car and car parts lying about. The trail now follows an old road. You'll see more car parts and at 1.6 miles a car overturned against a tree, as if the car ran off the road and the driver just left it there.

The lake is now below the trail on the right. At 2.1 miles, the trail turns left to leave the roadbed for an ascent of Shuckstack Ridge. Ascend on a footpath paralleling a stream on the right. Turn to cross the stream and continue steeply up to the ridgeline at 2.3 miles and then continue ascending along the other side of the ridge. You'll cross a small stream and then a wide shallow stream at 2.7 miles. The trail climbs steeply, and then down to a stream crossing. Then up to cross the next ridge. The trail from here is a series of ups and downs, crossing parallel ridges with usually small streams in the coves between.

At 5.5 miles, you'll switchback right and left to descend to a junction with the Lost Cove Trail beside Lost Cove Creek. To the right, the Lost Cove Trail descends 0.2 mile to campsite #90 on the embayment of Eagle Creek. The trail continues straight to the lake edge, but a turn to the left takes you through the campsite to a ford of Lost Cove Creek and beyond to the beginning of the Eagle Creek Trail. The Lakeshore Trail ends there; plans call for a new segment of trail to extend the trail east along the lake to connect with the other completed section of the Lakeshore Trail that ends at Proctor.

At the junction of the Lakeshore Trail with the Lost Cove Trail, turn left to stay on the loop. You'll ascend upstream along Lost Cove Creek and in the next half mile ford the creek six times. You'll cross a seventh time at 6.3 miles, but by now the creek has branched and you can get across by rockhopping. The trail then curves left through campsite #91 and continues to follow Lost Cove Creek while ascending Twentymile Ridge.

The trail descends to a junction with an old road and then bears right to continue ascending. You'll still be following Lost Cove Creek and will cross it and its small tributaries several times on the way up. At 7.8 miles, the trail cuts across the head of Lost Cove Creek and climbs steeply with several switchbacks to reach Sassafras Gap on Twentymile Ridge and a junction of trails at 9.0 miles. Straight ahead, the Twentymile Trail descends the other side of the ridge 5.0 miles to the Twentymile Access. To the right the AT leads to the crest of the Smokies at Doe Knob in 3.0 miles. Turn left on the AT to stay on the loop.

You'll ascend along the ridge to a junction at 9.3 miles with the AT continuing right and a side trail to the left that leads 0.1 mile to the Shuckstack firetower. You'll find there a chimney remaining from the watchman's house beside the firetower, which affords panoramic views of this southern portion of the park and Fontana Lake. The firetower was constructed in 1932.

From this junction, continue south on the AT, descending steeply from the Shuckstack summit. The trail switchbacks left at 9.5 miles and continues descending to a relatively level section of trail beginning at 9.7 miles. Watch for a natural rock wall on the left covered in lichen. As you continue out the ridgeline, the trail has some ups and downs until a steep descending stretch at 10.5 miles. At 12.8 miles the trail swings right around a large oak with an AT blaze and drops off the ridgeline. It's now a steady descent back to the road and trailhead at 13.0 miles.

**View from the Shuckstack**

233

# 64 Twentymile/Long Hungry Ridge Trails

7.5 miles one way
(Twentymile Creek Cascades 0.6 mile one way)
(Gregory Bald 8.2 miles one way)
Difficult
Elevation gain: 3300 ft.
Cautions: Stream crossings, steady climb
Campsites: #93, #92
Connections: Wolf Ridge, Twentymile Loop, Appalachian,
Gregory Bald Trails

**Attractions**: These trails combine with the Gregory Bald and Wolf Ridge Trails to make another of the outstanding loop backpacks in the park. For a good dayhike, you can take the Twentymile Loop Trail to the Wolf Ridge Trail.

**Trailhead**: From the Abrams Creek Access, head southeast on US129 and turn left on NC28 to the Twentymile Access on the left at 18.0 miles. From the Fontana Dam Access, stay on NC28 and you'll reach the Twentymile Access on the right at 5.2 miles. After turning into Twentymile, park just past the ranger station.

**Description**: Walk up the gravel road and pass around a gate blocking further vehicle access. Continue up the road, paralleling Twentymile Creek on your right. At 0.4 mile, the confluence of Moore Springs Branch with Twentymile Creek is barely noticeable amid thick rhododendron. At 0.5 mile you'll cross Moore Springs Branch on a wide bridge and encounter a junction with the Wolf Ridge Trail to the left. This is the other end of a 15-mile backpacking loop that leads up the Twentymile and Long Hungry Ridge Trails, crosses Gregory Bald, and then descends on the Wolf Ridge Trail. Stay on the Twentymile Trail to the right.

Soon a side trail leads to the right to Twentymile Creek Cascades, where the creek stairsteps down a drop in the creekbed. Continue straight up the old road, probably once an old railbed
234

where narrow-gauge trains hauled timber out of the mountains. You'll cross Twentymile Creek on bridges two times before coming to campsite #93 at 1.8 miles. Just beyond, you'll cross the creek on a bridge again and then a bridge over a small tributary at 2.2 miles. Just beyond this crossing, Twentymile Creek glides down a long rock slide. At 2.3 miles a stream passes under the road, and at 2.5 miles and 2.6 miles the road crosses Twentymile Creek on bridges again.

The road now parallels a smaller creek on your right as it ascends to a junction at 3.0 miles. To the right, the Twentymile Trail eventually reaches the AT at Sassafras Gap in 2.0 miles. To the left, the Twentymile Loop Trail leads 3.0 miles to the Wolf Ridge Trail; by taking this loop trail and then Wolf Ridge Trail back to the parking area, you can do a 7.5-mile dayhike. Take the Long Hungry Ridge Trail, which is the middle fork at this junction.

The Long Hungry Ridge Trail initially follows an old railbed that descends to cross a small stream on a bridge. You'll then drop off the old roadway to rockhop Proctor Branch at 3.2 miles and then climb back up to the roadway. The trail soon begins paralleling Twentymile Creek once more. You'll cross two small tributaries where there were short bridges, but only the spanning beams remain, to eventually reach campsite #92 at 4.3 miles. The trail curves left through the campsite to cross Greer Branch; you'll have to rockhop. You'll then have an uphill walk to a crossing of Twentymile Creek itself at 4.6 miles; you'll find an easier rockhop to your left. An old train car wheel lies to the left at this crossing, if no one has moved it by the time you get there.

The trail then climbs steeply, paralleling Rye Patch Branch. You'll cross a small stream and then Rye Patch Branch at 4.9 miles. The trail then begins a steep ascent with several switchbacks to top Long Hungry Ridge at 6.8 miles at Rye Patch, a swatch of grass surrounded by trees. The trail makes a right turn here to then follow the ridge to the crest of the Smokies at 7.5 miles and a junction with the Gregory Bald Trail. To the right, you can reach the AT in 2.0 miles. To the left, you'll pass in 0.1 mile the Gregory Ridge Trail on the right that leads down to Cades Cove, and then in another 0.6 mile you'll cross Gregory Bald to connect with the Wolf Ridge Trail at 1.2 miles.

# 65 Wolf Ridge Trail

6.5 miles one way
(Parsons Bald 5.8 miles one way)
(Gregory Bald 7.0 miles one way)
Moderate
Elevation gain: 3300 ft.
Cautions: Creek crossings, steady ascent
Campsites: #95, #13
Connections: Twentymile, Twentymile Loop,
Gregory Bald Trails

**Attractions**: This trail ascends to the Smokies crest and combines with the Gregory Bald, Long Hungry Ridge, and Twentymile Trails to form a good backpacking loop.

**Trailhead**: Follow the directions in Trail #64 to the Twentymile Access and walk up the Twentymile Trail 0.5 mile to the beginning of the Wolf Ridge Trail on the left.

**Description**: Turn left off the Twentymile Trail to begin your walk on the Wolf Ridge Trail. At first the trail ascends along an old roadbed through a mixed forest of hardwood, hemlock, and rhododendron while paralleling Moore Springs Branch on your left. The creek contains picturesque spillways and slides. Notice at 0.2 mile a slot of water that falls a few feet, hits a large boulder, and makes a right-angle turn.

At 0.3 mile the trail crosses Moore Springs Branch on a long footbridge. You'll cross again on footbridges at 0.4 mile and at 0.5 mile. Then at 0.7 mile you'll cross again, but this time you've run out of bridges and must wade the creek. At 0.9 mile, you'll ford the creek again, and continue up the roadway that may be an old railroad bed.

The trail reaches a junction at 1.0 mile with the Twentymile Loop Trail that leads right 3.0 miles to connect with the Twentymile Trail. This route makes for a good day loop hike of 7.5 miles that returns along the Twentymile Trail to the trailhead.

Curve left at this junction to stay on the Wolf Ridge Trail while now paralleling upstream Dalton Branch, a tributary of Moore Springs Branch, on your left. You'll cross several small streams as you ascend to a sharp right turn at campsite #95 at 2.0 miles. From the campsite, you'll now make an ascent of Wolf Ridge. At 2.9 miles, the trail crosses a small stream that falls steeply to your right. You'll cross another small stream at 3.2 miles and then ascend to pass left around a point as you move to the other side of Wolf Ridge. You'll now parallel a small stream up a hollow to the ridgeline at 3.4 miles.

From here up, you'll now ascend along the top of Wolf Ridge as it leads up to the Smokies crest. The trail makes several switchbacks and sharp curves on the way. At 5.8 miles, you'll ascend through a boundary zone of small trees and then emerge onto Parsons Bald, an open area of grass and shrubs. This is a good place to lay out lunch that should have fewer people than nearby Gregory Bald. In the early 1800s, crowds once gathered here for revivals, and so the name "Parsons Bald," although some say it was named for a man who helped build a turnpike through the region in 1829.

The trail then descends from the summit of Parsons Bald, reentering the forest but still with luxurious grass on the forest floor. You'll reach the end of the trail at Sheep Pen Gap at 6.5 miles and connect with the Gregory Bald Trail and campsite #13. Straight ahead, the Gregory Bald Trail leads down to Sams Gap on the Parson Branch Road out of Cades Cove. To the right, the trail leads up 0.5 mile to Gregory Bald. By passing over Gregory Bald to the junction of the Long Hungry Ridge Trail, you can return to the beginning of the Wolf Ridge Trail by following the Long Hungry Ridge Trail down to the Twentymile Trail that you takes back to your starting point.

**The Smokies**

238

# Selected References

Brewer, Alberta and Carson. 1975. *Valley So Wild, A Folk History*. Knoxville: East Tennessee Historical Society.

Brewer, Carson. 1981. *A Wonderment of Mountains, The Great Smoky Mountains*. Knoxville: Tenpenny Publishing.

Campbell, Carlos C., et al. 1977. *Great Smoky Mountains Wildflowers*. Knoxville: The University of Tennessee Press.

Campbell, Carlos, C. 1960. *Birth of a National Park in the Great Smoky Mountains*. Knoxville: UT Press.

Dykeman, Wilma, and Jim Stokely. 1978. *Highland Homeland, The People of the Great Smokies*. Washington, D.C.: U.S. Department of the Interior.

Dunn, Durwood. 1988. *Cades Cove, The Life and Death of a Southern Appalachian Community, 1818-1937*. Knoxville: The University of Tennessee Press.

Finger, John R. 1984. *The Eastern Band of Cherokees, 1819-1900*. Knoxville: The University of Tennessee Press.

Frome, Michael. 1980. *Strangers in High Places, The Story of the Great Smoky Mountains*. Knoxville: UT Press.

Great Smoky Mountains National Park. 1981. *Great Smoky Mountains*, Handbook 112. Washington, D.C.: U.S. Department of the Interior.

Harris, Ann G. 1977. "Great Smoky Mountains National Park," pp. 261-271 in *Geology of National Parks*, 2nd Edition. Dubuque, Iowa: Kendall/Hunt Publishing Company.

Kephart, Horace. 1922. *Our Southern Highlanders*. Knoxville: The University of Tennessee Press.

King, Duane H., ed. 1979. *The Cherokee Nation, A Troubled History*. Knoxville: The University of Tennessee Press.

King, Philip B., et al. 1968. *Geology of the Great Smoky Mountains National Park, Tennessee and North Carolina*, Geological Survey Paper. Washington, D.C.: U.S. GPO.

Luther, Edward T. 1977. *Our Restless Earth*. Knoxville: The University of Tennessee Press.

Shields, A. Randolph. 1977. *The Cades Cove Story*. Gatlinburg: Great Smoky Mountains Natural History Association.

# Trail Index

**Trail** (*hiking trail only*),  **page numbers**

242

# Addresses and Phone Numbers

Great Smoky Mountains National Park
Gatlinburg, Tennessee 37738, 615/436-1200
Backcountry Reservation Office, 615/436-1231

*For environmental education programs and field courses and hiking*

Great Smoky Mountains Institute at Tremont
Great Smoky Mountains National Park
Townsend, Tennessee 37882
615/448-6709

Smoky Mountain Field School
Non-Credit Programs
600 Henley St., Suite 105
University of Tennessee
Knoxville, Tennessee 37902

Great Smoky Mountains Hiking Club
P.O. Box 1454
Knoxville, Tennessee 37901

*For publications*

Great Smoky Mountains Natural History Association
Rt. 2, Box 572B
Gatlinburg, Tennessee 37738, 615/436-7318

*For Horseback Riding*

Cades Cove, 615/448-6286
Cosby, 615/623-6981
Sugarlands (McCarter's), 615/436-5354
Smokemont, 704/497-2373
Greenbrier (Smoky Mountains), 615/436-5634

*For Accommodations*

LeConte Lodge
250 Apple Valley Road
Sevierville, Tennessee  37862
615/429-5704

Bryson City Chamber of Commerce
P.O. Box 509
Bryson City, North Carolina  28713
704/488-3681

Cherokee Visitor Center
P.O. Box 460
Cherokee, North Carolina  28719
1-800-438-1601 or 704/497-9195

Fontana Village Resort
P.O. Box 68
Fontana Dam, North Carolina  28733
1-800-849-2258 or 704/498-2211

Gatlinburg Chamber of Commerce
P.O. Box 527, 520 Parkway
Gatlinburg, Tennessee  37738
1-800-438-8080 or 1-800-822/1998 or 615/430-4148

Pigeon Forge Department of Tourism
P.O. Box 1390
Pigeon Forge, Tennessee  37868
1-800-251-9100 or 615/453-8574

Smoky Mountains Visitors Bureau
1104 E. Lamar Alexander Parkway
Maryville, Tennessee  37801
615/984-6200

# Other Books from Mountain Laurel Place

### *The Best of the Big South Fork*
(2nd Edition)
A hiker's guide to the Big South Fork National River and Recreation Area in Tennessee and Kentucky. $6.95

### *The South Cumberland and Fall Creek Falls*
A hiker's guide to the South Cumberland Recreation Area and Fall Creek Falls State Park in Tennessee. $6.95

### *Historic Knoxville and Knox County*
(Bicentennial Edition)
A walking and touring guide to the historic city center, neighborhoods, parks, and back roads of this Tennessee city and county. Sale $6.95 (Regular $8.95)

## Order Form

Send check or money order to:

**Mountain Laurel Place**

P.O. Box 3001                   Telephone
Norris, TN 37828                615/494-8121

| Title | Price | Quantity | Total |
|-------|-------|----------|-------|
| *The Best of the BSF*, 2nd Ed. | $6.95 | | |
| *The South Cum. and FCF* | $6.95 | | |
| *The Best of the GSM* | $10.95 | | |
| *Historic Knoxville* | $6.95 | | |
| | | Subtotal | |
| | | Tenn. residents add 7.75% sales tax | |
| | | Shipping and handling* | |
| | | Total enclosed | |

*Add $1.50 for shipping/handling if ordering one book or for each book if separate mailing is requested. We pay for shipping/handling if more than one book is ordered and mailed in one shipment to the same the address.

Ship to _____

Address _____

_____

Items offered subject to availability. Prices subject to change without notice.